Success of Evil.

ELEMENTS OF SUCCESS

IN THE

KINGDOM OF EVIL.

BY

A. S. KEDZIE,

PASTOR OF THE CONGREGATIONAL CHURCH IN DEXTER, MICHIGAN.

BOSTON:

CONGREGATIONAL PUBLISHING SOCIETY.

1873.

ALFRED MUDGE & SON, PRINTERS,
34 SCHOOL STREET, BOSTON.

Dedication.

TO

TWO NAMESAKES,

WHO IN THE OTHER LEARNED PROFESSIONS

HAVE SHOWN THAT

LIFE CAN BE AN ELEMENT OF SUCCESS

IN THE

KINGDOM OF CHRIST,

THIS VOLUME IS DEDICATED BY

THE AUTHOR.

PREFACE.

It is thought the following discussion can find fit place in the present state of religious inquiry, and may help to a clearer view of the contest which fills so largely past ages and the present. No one can understand society in the particulars and aggregate of its action till he finds it a strife between opposite moral forces; nor till then can understand the meaning of history.

What is here offered only starts an inquiry which the Christian thinker will push further. Attempt is made to handle only the more obvious and proximate Elements of Sin's Success. Others, as efficient, lie not far off: as, Hierarchism, Political Corruption, Materialism, Secret Organizations, Corrupt Literature, Weak Tone of the Moral Convictions expressed in Civil Law, and the Antagonism held between Capital and Labor. Of these, the Author has not treated because incompetent to do so to his satisfaction, and because thereby unable to keep the discussion within desired limits.

The standpoint is historic, not prophetic. Evil is held to have such Success as history and the present condition of society certify, — only partial, because weak compared with opposing strength, yet terrible hitherto and now. This meagre review of Sin's forces and modes gives no full view of the contest; nor can this be had till sight is gained by the Elements of Final and Triumphant Success found in the Kingdom of Christ, some thoughts on which will be offered as soon as the press of other duties permits.

A. S. K.

Dowagiac, Michigan, January, 1873.

CONTENTS.

SUCCESS OF EVIL.

CHAPTER I.

STATEMENT OF THE CASE.

ACCEPTING Moral Evil as a fact, we inquire into its success hitherto. The origin of Evil, so long debated, is perhaps as well understood as it can be, till studied amid the disclosures of a future state. Passing that by, we take the situation as we find it, and raise the question, Why Evil, against reason and revelation, against the best welfare of soul and society, should come to a success so respectable? Even apart from its bearing on the destiny of the soul, simply as a fact of society, Evil in its extent and success hitherto is worthy of profoundest study.

The destructive tendencies of Moral Evil, its oppugnance to all that reason affirms and revelation discloses as good, may be readily seen in every show Evil makes of itself. Religion pronounces what experience has clearly demonstrated: that the duty is also the interest of men; that both for the individual and for society, it is better to be just, honorable, and benevolent, than to be unjust, base, and cruel; that the laws of God are the only modes of gaining highest welfare; that it is folly to sacrifice an endless future of good for present gratifications which leave a sting of regret. It is easy to show that no man should subject the high aspirations of his soul to low passions and gross animalism; and men from the first, through all generations and lands, should have striven for the highest nobility in intelligence and virtue.

When we turn away from these grand possibilities lying before men, and look at the record of history, or at the present state of the world, the extent of Evil overwhelms the mind with wonder and sadness. To get any intelligent and profound conviction of the sinfulness of the world, fills the mind with dread and horror. Why do not the nations arrest their mad folly, cover themselves with sackcloth, and mourn for the miseries they have brought upon themselves? Who can look upon the wave of guilt rolling down through the ages and deluging the earth to-day, bearing to all lands and homes the wretchedness inflicted by selfishness, hatred, ambition, avarice, intemperance, libertinism, war, slavery, and their long list of crimes, and not, in anguish of heart, groan out, This is dreadful? Then, if he shall make closer inspection, searching into the interior experience of men for all manifold diversities and shadings of guilt and sorrow, what intensity of language can utter his convictions!

He has no eyes who does not see this misery; no heart who does not weep over it. If such can be found, there sin shows its completest work, which is the completest wreck. If worse were done with humanity, what else could it be than to have sin rage and ravage as now?

Were Evil found only in some obscure corner of the earth, where frigid clime and niggard nature had pinched man with their sorest stress, or where ignorance had kept in concealment the grand possibilities of human nature, or only in some particular age in which it had stood out as an anomaly beyond all reach of solution, it might have passed as a simple marvel. But it has overspread the earth, in Christian lands and heathen, in extremest climes, and where man finds best conditions for development. It has occupied all the spaces of history, even where clearest light has shone and highest civilization been reached. Even when culture hides the grossness of sin, it is only to give it new fascination, power, and prevalence in highest levels of society. It pervades society as an atmosphere, surging like a storm around all homes, everywhere scattering misery and keeping alive wretchedness. It wastes like a demon, letting no heart escape its sting, and multiplying its thrusts with the days, till all hearts ache and all eyes weep. Down through all ages, abroad in all lands, so it has been and it is to-day.

There may be said to be a Kingdom of Evil, as there is a Kingdom of Righteousness: each opposed to the other; each organized and in contest for ascendency. So in this world: how much further, it matters not at present. The Kingdom of Righteousness is organized in the Divine Sovereignty at its head, in its laws of morals, mind, and matter, in the church, and all just institutions of society. In history are seen its organized procedures. So the Kingdom of Evil, in its historical record and witnessed working, is best understood by supposing a similar organization, less perfect, since its very principles forbid wise administration and true loyalty. It has no great truths or sweet affinities to bind men together in constancy and fellowship.

Yet such a vast aggregation of bad minds, however false to each other, having similar aims, come into modes of action which are an organized method, an institute. Nothing can be done so generally and continuously without falling into an organizing method. Knowledge and skill gained by long experience give efficiency in wrong as in right. If, thereby, some revolters against the Divine Rule, of such transcendent genius and reckless apostacy as to dare rivalship with God, though often supplanted by intrigue of others, should nevertheless perpetuate an administration under one dynasty or another, imbue others with their spirit, inspire methods of wrong action, or merely provoke imitation in evil, it would necessarily involve an organization, not only as necessary to its ends, but because organized methods could not be excluded.

Evil, as it works in this world, affords illustration. When tyrants get into power, possible even in democracies; when stock-jobbers override all principles of commercial integrity; when leaders of fashion give new impulse, larger expenditure, and a fresh abandonment to spendthrift ways, by capriciously changing the costumes of society, its style of living, and ways of amusement; or, in a particular community, some gain influence, inaugurate new methods of corruption, and set many in a drift to ruin, — they act upon a method which shows organization, even if not consciously planned. Such efficiency is shown, such wrong sway given to public morals, as bespeaks strength. Things are done, ends accomplished, that lie beyond the reach of individual effort. The modes they inaugurate become an institute of society.

The Scriptures give warrant for what we would infer from observation. The principalities and powers, the rulers of the darkness of this world, spiritual wickedness in high places, against which the Kingdom of Righteousness wrestles in warfare ; the prince of the power of the air, the spirit that now worketh in the children of disobedience, whatever more they may be, indicate a malign force and agency, whose directness of aim, so long continued, necessarily involves an organization, however often disrupted as to personal administration by intestine disloyalty.

The Kingdom of Evil has not yet had full hearing. However possible at any time its subjects may be put to writhing under conviction of their wrong, yet respite of condemnation is also possible, as human experience in sin shows. Such are the delusions of sin, that resort may be had even to justification. And in this we can conceive that autonomy without law may be the principle of that Kingdom; that in revolt against Divine Rule, they advocate and defend the right of each to follow his own will, even to the extent of a disintegrating individualism. If this should seem to take away the foundation of organization, it befits the inconsistencies of sin to disown the application of its own principles, and if power can be grasped, to maintain organization by the severities of tyranny. But however held together, it is in the nature of the Kingdom of Evil to organize. If there be no personal chieftain at its head, no allegiance, loyalty, or order in Evil, yet even autonomic anarchy must have modes of action, varied, yet only to be repeated and thereby becoming a method. The fixed array of bad minds necessarily holds them to methods that are organic.

Whatever Omnipotence might do in clearing the universe of all resistance, such use of his power seems not to be God's method. He treats his creatures according to the natures he has given them. For dead matter he has physical force; animals he handles by imperious instincts; but moral beings, made to be governed by truth, to be ruled by right, to be won by love, to be warned by the preannounced consequences of revolt, and made to have fellowship of thought and feeling with himself, he addresses as standing on that high level. He gives them autonomy under law, refuses to push them with compulsions, but handles them with a gentleness that would make them great. And when the bad have reached eternal confirmation in character, as all moral beings must, it may be one of the necessary pains of their hell that he will not let them drop from this high dignity.

Constituted of such elements, imbued with such a spirit, and organized on such principles, clearly the Kingdom of Evil should have dragged from the beginning and have come to a speedy and ignominious failure. In whatever world found, it is an unpardonable impertinence. In opposition to truth and right, against reason and conscience, opposed to best welfare both of soul and society, perverting all highest powers in man; but, most of all, disputing the legitimacy of God's Rule, contemning his justice, rejecting his love, trying his patience, grieving his heart, and crucifying his Son; such a Kingdom of Evil not only should not be, but, existing from the first, should have proved an abortion, and not even come to any conspicuousness of failure. And when great enough to be in full opposition to God's Kingdom of Righteousness, its management by finite minds should have doomed it to sure and speedy overthrow.

Never did results so disappoint expectation. Instead of abortive failure, the Kingdom of Evil has come to a success not only respectable, but as nigh perfect as the infirmity of finiteness permits to anything it touches. If, in the record of history, any success is to be found, it is in the growth and sway of this Kingdom. Not even the Kingdom of Righteousness makes show of such success. Its greater success is yet in promise and prophecy. Whatever faith may see in the deeper under-currents of history, the plainest things upon its record are the doings and triumphs of the Kingdom of Evil. Here we see moving the masses of Earth's population; their intensified activities; their interest, occupancy, and complete absorption. When the Epic of Evil comes to be written in quantities, numbers, and achievements, history will furnish material for showing a success greater than the human mind has yet conceived.

CHAPTER II.

THE SITUATION.

MAN has the power of non-consent. It does not therefore impugn the omnipotence and benevolence of God that sin exists. Certainly, God desires no such result. It is against his will, against every attribute of his infinitely pure and beneficent character. He has created moral and accountable souls, incident to the peril of sin through non-consent, rather than create only material things to be governed and run as machines under the law of absolute force, or to make merely animals to be handled by imperious instincts. Himself an intelligent and moral being, it would be no sufficient pleasure to him to have merely a kingdom of matter, though the worlds move in harmony inconceivably beautiful, or to rule only a brute creation.

He has created beings that can have fellowship of thought and feeling with himself, capable of moral and intellectual reciprocities. If from this high level they fall, he may still have it, as an end sought, to bring them under the sway of such principles, on through such an experience, as will finally clear them from the dominion and damage of sin, if they will only consent; without which, from the nature of the case, it would be impossible.

Not the final completion of God's plan, but the present situation, is now the matter for study. Sin embodied in sinners, personated in so many fallen beings, has become a tremendous power, pervading society, corrupting it, blending and bewildering the minds of men, practically an organized force, a Kingdom of Evil opposed to the Kingdom of Christ. To maintain this opposition, to open some chance of success, what fashioning of our surroundings might we naturally and reasonably expect the forces of Evil would inaugurate and maintain? Before taking up that question, let us stay a little to fix in mind some conviction of the personality of sin, — to many a mere abstraction, if not a myth.

There is something tremendously real in this Kingdom of Sin, seen geographically or historically. All the world's most prominent affairs, its outward and visible concerns, sin has shaped and handled through all the ages of history. To-day, sin in the main holds them in possession the world over. Here and there a rare Christian man is found, who has brought all his affairs into the Kingdom of Christ. Not his heart alone, but his entire powers; not his Sabbaths, but his week-days also; not his religious observances, but as totally his daily toil, — he holds and handles for Christ. Maintaining his abode or removing elsewhere, the whole line of business he shall follow, its method and extent, his action in social life, everything with him is determined by a conscious and intelligent reference to the bearing it will have on his personal piety, the religious welfare of his family, the success of the church, and the salvation of the world. But the world knows not such men, and may be even incredulous as to their existence, — counting a description of such characters a fiction of fancy. The men of the world are in no level where they can see Christians; so their denials are natural enough. Even when admitted to be legitimate and normal characters, how few they seem, — wellnigh lost beyond discovery in the vast aggregate of humanity; in any assemblage, how few; in how many, none at all!

The great bulk of humanity belongs to the Kingdom of Sin. These are they who transact the vast aggregate of the world's business, hold its capital, prosecute its enterprises, push its adventures, incite its industries, fill its offices, and control its government. It is with these interests that the newspapers are filled. These enterprises occupy the world's incessant talk. Far away into forests, deep down into mines, abroad on the oceans, or mid steam and smoke and din of factories, these interests are pushed. Over broad territories, along the valleys, up the hill-sides into the interior of the mountains, and far off into the depth of the sea, with insane eagerness and crazy fanaticism the enterprises of selfish and sinful greed are pushed. A sad spectacle! grandest show of folly! — relieved of sadness, to those who feel it, only by the mitigating conviction of final overrulement to the true ends of humanity and God!

Men go eagerly into these enterprises of gain and

into these schemes of ambition as into pursuit of pleasure. Energy is stimulated, time used; what else would be weariness and a burden brings gratification. Curiosity is whetted, thought is quickened, ingenuity put to task, evolution of risks watched with eager interest, hopes brighten and fade to brighten again, success comes within reach, and victories are gained. How satisfactory! Life within such bounds seems to them full-orbed.

And they not merely rest satisfied in these ways of worldly delight, content to have all their powers put to such use, and putting to such use all things within their control; but they refuse to be turned out of their ways, to be lifted to any other level, even if countenanced by the company of entire humanity. They would not have all the world wake up to-morrow Christian, — as earnestly and devoted Christian as the holiest ever were. They would feel awkward, unassured, uncertain how matters would turn; what success they would likely reach. No, they want affairs to go in their wonted ways. They have a use for the world and humanity as they now find them. Their plans are adjusted to the present state of affairs. Present conditions meet their wants. How many, for example, live by the pride of others!

Take out of commerce what simply ministers to pride; shut up all manufactories which supply such material; turn adrift the artisans thus employed; withdraw the capital thus invested; and how would the world's affairs be deranged! Many live by the world's passions and lusts. Take simply two, intemperance and licentiousness, still leaving a large list. In gratification of these two, how much capital and how many persons find employment! Crush out intemperance and licentiousness to-day, and in what deranged state would the world's affairs be found on the morrow!

With what cruel determination is the love of gain prosecuted. If helpless operatives are in body crushed down to the level next above starvation, and their minds to a still lower level; if the lives of men are imperilled by insecure railroads, dangerous factories or steamers, or in coal mines with only one entrance; if the construction of a Panama railroad within set time costs many lives to the mile, — what matter? ask these men intent on gain. And the same questions they ask, if their ways of gain bring all the ruin which gambling, intemperance, and harlotry can work.

Take the lust of power, political and ecclesiastical, as recorded in history. If, by impressment to fill the ranks of armies, families are separated; if battles leave the ground strewed with dead and dying; if countries are desolated, cities sacked; if starvation and plague follow in the train, — what matter? if the throne of empire is only reached! What if men are imprisoned for their faith, put to the rack, or burned at the stake? so that hierarchy can hold sway!

Sin a myth? The kingdom of sin a chimera? What more tremendously real and more portentous of evil can be found? In such a kingdom every sinner is a citizen, thoroughly loyal to its principles, determined that its policy shall not be interfered with, that its enterprises shall go on and its power be maintained. They have put all their investments into it, bound all interests to it. Nothing would so stir their wrath, or provoke them to such resistance, as an array of Christian influences, threatening a speedy overthrow of the Kingdom of Evil. It would outdo the ten persecutions paganism brought against the early Christian church.

There is more in the Kingdom of Evil than the extent of its business and the hostility of its spirit. No full sense can be got of its reality without looking at its organic completeness. Were it disintegrated bulk, it would present stout resistance, like an impassable snow-drift to a railway train. But it has correlations, affiliations, and adhesions that give it strength. It has an unscrupulous coherence, is not troubled with being particular, but accepts whatever will debauch and ruin men, whether by little or much. Custom has established methods in the conduct of business, pervading all its ranges, yet clearly seen to be in the interests of sin. The world expects to violate its own rules of conduct. Usage gives sin respectability. Custom gives strength, as drill does to an army. The wonted ways of the world are an organizing force in the Kingdom of Evil.

As in business so in social life. Its customs open ways of tampering with temperance, veracity, and virtue; so come drunkenness, embezzlement, and seduction. Fashion, another organizing element in society, helps in the same way. Stated in abstract generality, this in look amounts to little. Could we gather up the published and unpublished illustrations found in any month's history, see the instances of ruin by intemperance, by frauds, by blighted affections, and seductions, for which the way was prepared by the fashions and customs of society, it would be obvious how these had become elements of organization in the Kingdom of Evil. Tricks, deceits, knaveries in business, cheats in manufacture and deal are excused because of custom. Affections are tampered with in social life, purity sullied, the imagination corrupted, passions inflamed, and the young ruined by customs of intercourse, by fashions in dress, by talk, demeanor, flirtations, late hours, promiscuous assemblies in ball-rooms, and in ways too numerous for recital. In these what sin has not found excuse?

Further on there is more. Methods devised and customs adopted in politics to give utterance to public sentiment, as in the caucus system, are perverted by neglect of some and chicanery of others to personal ambition and party corruption. So in legislatures, and even in courts of justice, defences of liberty and right are made to shield crimes and set criminals free. Wrong claims rights in this world, and even respectability. In civil and social life it has taken possession of custom. The usages of politics, jurisprudence, commerce, manufactures, and of trade, the fashions of social life and its modes of intercourse, have been appropriated by the Kingdom of Evil in accomplishing its ends. Herein it has an organic completeness, without which it would have only the weakness to which it is entitled.

Such is that Kingdom of Evil, which is in possession of the world, and justifies its right of possession by long inheritance. A Kingdom of Evil it is, which could not have been excluded, save by a necessity which would have excluded the opposing Kingdom of Righteousness, by remanding us to the control of absolute force, as are the materialities of nature. A Kingdom of Evil it is, organized, resistant, consenting to no encroachment, and restricted from universal prevalence only by the oppósing Kingdom of Christ.

The question arises, How comes this Kingdom of Evil to such success? Existing under the disadvantage of being against reason, conscience, justice, and righteousness, against all that conserves, blesses, and beautifies society, against all that exalts and ennobles the soul; opposed to all the securities of business, to the growth of substantial prosperity, and to tranquillity under civil law; militant against the soul's eternal welfare; in conflict with God's Kingdom of Righteousness, joy, peace, and salvation,—how comes the Kingdom of Evil to a success so respectable and pervasive? In other words, put to organizing such a kingdom, what elements would one incorporate in it to give it success?

It would be a cheap answer to say, Secure the fall of our race into sin, and the success of the Kingdom of Evil is secured. We wish to carry this discussion to a remove from this central point, to bring it nearer to the consciousness and experience of men. Indeed, the question is not, how men came into their present position, — whether by the fall of our first parents, or by sinning in some former and forgotten state of existence, — nor what their degree of debasement. All questions, as to how the Kingdom of Evil came to be, are passed by. We simply inquire as to the facts of actual history. We look into our surroundings to find sedatives by which men are made content with the life, and stimulants by which they are prompted to the courses they pursue. We inquire for the elements of success in the Kingdom of Evil.

CHAPTER III.

STIFLED CONVICTION OF IMMORTALITY.

ONE element of success would be incorporated in the Kingdom of Evil by banishing a practical and controlling faith in a future state of existence. Let the horizon of life shut down close around us; so that, beyond the circumference of this world and the goal of the grave, there was nothing with which we had to do; that the matters of practical concern with us lie within such narrow boundary, and few forces of God's Kingdom of Righteousness, none of its saving influences, would reach us. In such unbelief as to the future state we would be in best condition to take readily to all the incentives and indulgences sin might offer.

If this great party, this malign, portentous, and tremendously real Kingdom of Sin, that plies so strenuous an oppósition to the Kingdom of God, could only succeed in banishing all practical belief in immortality, men would be in a state of ready acceptance to all the proposals of sin that did not involve immediate danger. And minds unaccustomed to any outlook upon immortality would be blinded to the remoter perils of sin that come in this life. These they cannot see, unless they look far enough into the soul's history to gain some vision of immortality.

But this denial or even obliviousness of a future state is not easily gained. To beget it, earnest longings have to be quenched and noble ambitions smitten down. No one, at all aware of the capacities of the soul, would consent to annihilation. The sick child that could not consent to die, because he wanted to see the days and know how the things go on, uttered an infantile feeling, whose maturity demands immortality. Sin can secure an imbrutement that shall quench high aspirations and the ambition to make the most of one's self. Souls can be narrowed, dwarfed, and let down to so low a level as to care only for what the senses use. Held in such conditions, no longing will be felt, no ambitions raised, stirring their hopes to take hold on immortality.

To have the conviction of immortality stifled, more than such debasement is needful. There needs to be a forgetfulness of the most obvious facts of our condition. The changes through which we here pass foretoken just so grand an issue. Comparing the helplessness of our infancy with the vigor of our maturity, we find it a law of human life that we pass through continuous changes, each constituting some new and richer development. Not more different from its callow state is the full-fledged bird, or the butterfly from the chrysalis, than mature age from infancy. Immortality only completes former progress. The strong probability of such an issue must be broken down before we can reach unbelief in a future state.

In like manner, all the arguments for immortality would have to be laid aside, doing violence not less to reason than to revelation. Curiosity, a hunger for knowledge, a desire to make the most of one's self, the divine instinct of immortality must be suppressed, and man degrade himself to the brute level, to banish belief in a future life. This is difficult of accomplishment, since, outside of revelation, there is so broad and firm a foundation for belief in a future state; all the more difficult, since there is a grand inspiration in the belief, which has much to do with every-day life.

Were we to look at the warrant there is for this belief, and at the place it is to fill in the main design and minutiæ of a man's life, we would say that he could not forget this transcendent fact of his condition, surely not for a day; that an ever-present conviction of it would run through his daily history, at least that it would have advisement with him at every turn in life. Considering the make of the soul, its history, surroundings, and prospects, it is difficult to see how a belief in immortality could be pushed aside or made inoperative.

Yet just this is to be done, if the Kingdom of Evil reach any success, make any room for itself, and work with any efficiency. In organizing a Kingdom of Evil for the ruin of souls and to stand militant against God's Kingdom of Salvation, a first and chief thing will be to stifle the conviction of immortality, so that it shall have no practical influence in the plans and procedures of life. This is necessary to a thoroughly organized Kingdom of Evil. If, every day, men had a deep conviction, that close at hand lies an immortal state which they were soon to enter, to find it what foregone life had made it; with such a clear outlook upon immortality, the enchantment of sin would be broken; there would be no room for the play of its incentives, no thirst for its stimulants, no chance for the arousal of its terrible passions, and no possibility for a day's forgetfulness of the soul's welfare.

But the Kingdom of Evil is in no such jeopardy. Somehow, in ways utterly inexplicable, yet surely, the sense of immortality is deadened, the conviction of a future state stifled. This is a fact of the human condition open to any one's observation. Men who by process of argument can readily be brought to affirm their undisputed belief in a future state, live through days and weeks without any thought of it. Such an one can go to the sanctuary and not say, Soon I shall be through with this; soon have in open vision the things I here so dimly see. Memorable days of the year, anniversaries of birth may come, and he not say to himself, Soon for me these will pass, and I go on to my eternal manhood. He may rise up from a bed of sickness, without thinking that sometime soon a very different result will ensue. He may watch a thousand sunsets without saying, Soon and surely the sun of my life will set. A thousand sunrisings may gladden his vision, and he not think to say, Some morning, soon, the light of an eternal day will shine around me. He lays plans without the conviction that others must complete them, and begins enterprises without thought that other hands must finish them when his lose their skill.

So we find it along the marts of business, in shops and stores, on the streets, and in the homes of men. This is the world in which they live, without thought or care for any other. The vast mass of minds is sunk too low to gain any so grand and inspiring an outlook. With the vast majority of men the sense of a future state is dead, the conviction of immortality stifled. Not a whisper of it in talk, not a thought of it in mind, nor a sense of it in the heart.

All this is not against the Bible merely, nor against the well-grounded convictions of nature, but against the oft-repeated witness of death. A man looks upon a neighbor's face in the coffin, without thought that the same or other neighbors will thus look upon his coffined remains. He helps lay a friend's body away tenderly in the tomb with no sense of the fact that the same service will soon be done for him. In the hands of men he can miss the dead without inquiring, How soon shall I be missed? Of those who die of disease, adult life is seldom reached without some predisposition to the disease which will close their earthly career. It may make unmistakable show of itself, as the agent of that coming transformation, and yet this premonitory suffering be traced to no issue. For years of life he travels in close companionship, perhaps in conflict, with his final conqueror, without thought of the result.

Nor against instinct of nature merely, or fact of

observation, is this delusion, this strange oblivion to the most momentous fact of the human condition; but equally is it against the most ennobling and entrancing inspiration that can stir a man. That the mystery of life is soon to be explained to him, he soon to be free from the body, and spirit with a universe to range in, soon to greet foregone friends and to see the Divine One, — if these grand realities, or possibilities, are not the most entrancing inspirations and stir not the noblest aspirations, what can he be than a brute, unless he be a stone?

Wisely organized is this Kingdom of Evil, with means adjusted to ends. It makes not only possible, but sure, the ruin it seeks. What might be counted impracticable, to seduce souls from loyalty to God and make them reckless of best welfare, it can do. The forces that control it have gathered up the wisdom of long ages and the skill of wide experience. They have taken possession of business, of pleasure, of all schemes of ambition and all enterprises of life, and have held these so persistently and closely before men, that they gain no practical insight into life's meaning, nor any outlook upon life's results. So they stumble on, hoodwinked, to whatever is entrancing or terrible in the near-by immortality.

Assuredly, with direct conduciveness to its end, works this Kingdom of Evil, shielding men from alarms, cutting off the most entrancing views of life, and suppressing the most quickening inspirations. Any system less than this would be nothing. Take away this one cheat, give all men a clear and daily outlook upon immortality, and at the end of a brief campaign the Kingdom of Evil would fall.

CHAPTER IV.

THE MINIFACTION OF SIN.

IT is conceivable that a man may have a profound respect for the Devil, using that term either as representing a malign personage, or as personifying the Powers of Evil. We can have a respect for what we do not approve. It may not even make a successful appeal to our admiration. In war, an enemy, though engaged in a wrong cause and defending false principles, may nevertheless show a heroism, intrepidity, and fortitude, that command our respect. Let enthusiasm call out large armies, which leave behind all the comforts of home, subject themselves to the hardships of camp life, to all the fatigues of march, pass bravely into battle, and there manfully strive for victory, not yielding till many a field is lost,— their deep convictions and daring courage command our respect.

In the war of the Rebellion, the Southern States assembled armies of such gigantic proportions, they sacrificed so much, held out so persistently against superior forces, were so undaunted in defeat, and extricated themselves so often from what threatened to be a total overthrow, that for their skill and bravery, at least, they commanded the respect of the world, and even of the North.

There is a greater Rebellion than that which our arms overthrew in bringing to naught the Southern Confederacy,— a Rebellion founded on more destructive principles and maintained against greater odds. In its contests physical force is not in place, else Omnipotence would speedily crush it. The adherents of each contesting party are held to allegiance only by choice, and can be brought over to the opposite side only by choice. It is a contest for moral ascendency.

The final issue has not come. We have waked into being in time to see the contest go on. In the history of the universe this is the era of war. The Kingdom of Righteousness and the Kingdom of Evil are in conflict for ascendency over every soul throughout the world. How much larger the field of conflict, we know not. This is the sublimest thing going on in the world; the most comprehensive, for it includes all things. Nothing is, nothing transpires, but as a part of this contest. Every man has his place in one of these kingdoms or the other. If it is not so in conscious intent, it is nevertheless so in fact. This contest is the grandest thing of historic record.

In such conditions, what might we expect to find? We inquire further for elements of success in the Kingdom of Evil. To stifle the conviction of immortality, might seem enough; yet there is more. No one nor a few elements of success fully meet the case. A Kingdom so thoroughly organized, of such wide sweep and far-reaching aims, can depend on no one element of success. What else might we expect to find?

The Minifaction of Sin. Let sin be held as a trifle; let the distinction between holiness and sin, between sinful and Christian life, be compounded, so that a man feels there is no difference between Christians and sinners, except that the former are a little more circumspect, if not hypocritical, and that man is established in the Kingdom of Evil. Multiply this, till an entire community is befogged in this blunder, and in that community the Kingdom of Evil is a success. Simply as a prudent economy in commercial and social relations, as a wiser policy for this life, men may forbid certain things and require others. So come commercial and social virtues. These may be chiefly to do well by themselves in this life. All this may be made, though very inconsistently, to harmonize with a denial of the difference between holiness and sin.

To deny this distinction, and for this to minify sin, to hold it as a trifle, is not easily done. Conscience is against it. That voice of God in the soul, whenever heard, proclaims an eternal and irreconcilable difference between holiness and sin. Reason consents not to such confounding of moral judgments. It affirms, not only that all significant conduct is either holy or sinful, right or wrong, but that the highest culmination of moral activity — the greatest thing a man can do — is a righteous or sinful act. Herein are the real and positive things of life.

The witnessed things of life, its current history,

deny and protest against this disposition to count sin a trifle. Take any well-defined instance of it: for example, follow through the history of intemperance, see all its sights of wretchedness, hear all its sounds of woe, weep over its miseries, tremble at its guilt, nauseate at its disgusts, be in horror at its cruelties, indignant at its wrongs, and vengeful at its crimes; and what is found in it? Nothing criminal, nothing revolting, cruel, horrible, or wretched, save as sin is in it. Take the one element of sin out of it, and there would be left no sufferings, no wrongs, cruelties, bestialities, or demonism.

Go from the freedom of society, this liberty of self-management, from the cheer of homes and the sweet affinities of fellowship, down to the restraints and repellancies of a penitentiary; and what makes the difference? Only sin, and the consequent handling men are compelled to give it. Sin can make any what these convicts are. Take the best men known, and the worst; and what makes the difference? Only sin. That worst man may have sinned not merely against God's moral law, but also against all laws for the training of mind, the management of the body, and the conservation of the social order; but as the worst man, he is only the man fullest of sin.

We all know something of war, — some by actual participation, all by reading and the anxieties we have felt. We know what hardships are met, what sufferings, yea, agonies, are endured on the march, in camp, on battle-field, in hospital, in Libby Prisons and Andersonvilles. In all these, what is the matter? Only sin. Take away wrong, sin acted out, and all these sufferings, cruelties, agonies, and horrors vanish.

We have not forgotten slavery; it cost us too much for that. What cruelties were endured, agonies peddled out, by men who went from one plantation to another to inflict lashes on those whose unsubdued humanity kept them in revolt against oppression; separation of families into returnless exile; ignorance which no education was permitted to relieve; hungerings of heart that must not be fed! Sin did all this.

Turning from sin as an organic force in society, to study it in individuals, its nature is found the same, and it is seen as difficult to be counted a trifle. A young man, the son of doting parents, at cost of much parental sacrifice, has qualified himself for business by a long, thorough, and expensive education. Loving hearts bore privation and hardship that he might go into the world's commercial marts competent to transact any intricate and responsible business. At length, leaving home with all fondest hopes centred upon him, he takes a responsible position in some mercantile house or bank, where large sums of money pass through his hands. For a while he meets the expectations of his employers and the hopes of his parents. But unknown to them he has fallen into evil company. A festive gathering of associates introduces wine and cards. For want of excitement they play for the supper. Heavier gambling comes naturally enough. His gambling debts cannot be paid without drawing salary which he has not yet earned. Soon he needs the lost salary and larger advances than he can earn; so he makes false entries on the ledger, and covers them with forged checks, which he vainly hopes to take up before they fall due or meet detection. The picture need not be drawn out in detail. It is familiar to readers of newspapers. Discovery is made; detection lays its hand upon him; he is pronounced a felon and sent to prison. All his bright hopes, that ran so far into the future, end in the darkness and gloom of the cell. In parents' hearts joy and hope are turned to grief and despair: a grief whose burden they must bear through life; a despair which only the hope of heaven can mitigate. Dishonesty did all this; and all the matter with dishonesty is, that it is sin.

What brighter or more beautiful gem has society than a gifted and highly-cultivated daughter, blushing into all the beauties of young maidenhood? And yet with what melancholy frequence has such an one, after long solicitation, given her too trustful love to a man that was not only seductive, but a seducer; who decoyed her to a house of assignation, only to thrust her into a degradation from which her own outraged feelings and the cruel verdict of society never permit her to rise. In the few years that mark her run to an early grave, what ages of woe are crowded, as she thinks what might have been! And the desolation of the home she has left no one can know till the destroyer comes to his. What wrought such ruin, brought such blight, turned so much sweetness into gall, so much hope into despair? Sin did it. Nothing else could.

A man is pronounced by the court a murderer. If he escape the gallows, it is only to pine away his life in solitary confinement; and no outsider can conceive the agony involved in that. But he cannot take all the curse of his crime into that cell. Part — O, how much! — is borne by that wife who testified so bravely for him, and who wept so sorrowfully on his shoulder when the verdict was given. What came into that house and sent that husband to such a doom, and that broken-hearted wife to go forth and find what the world has in store for a murderer's wife? Sin did it. Only sin could.

Take intemperance, gambling, adultery, murder, and the long list of crimes: see what they can do in wasting the fortunes, blasting the prospects, and crushing the hopes of individuals and their families: see what such crimes can do in society. More still; imagine, if possible, all the wretchedness and ruin they could effect, if unrestrained by law or gospel: and even then, gathering up all the world's woe, it will be found no adequate measure of the magnitude of sin. It reaches deeper than the understanding can fathom, further than the imagination can conceive.

Hurts and the keenest stings come not from crimes alone, but from sins which the civil law cannot touch. There is wrong and its consequent suffering in many a home; but all the instruments of civil law are too coarse and bungling to bring rectification or relief. A word, a look, even tones of voice, have stung deeper, left in the heart a heavier press of agony, than ever misfortune could. Frivolity, neglect, even heedlessness, have sent pain into the heart, to live there as long as it will beat.

Take the one fact of disappointment. "He is not the husband my heart took him for. O, what might have been!" "She is not the wife my mind had pictured, and my heart had craved. Now too late!" This son has not met the high hopes cherished through all the years of his growth. This daughter, so tenderly nourished, has proved a viper. This friend, leaned upon so confidently, has pierced hand and side. So disappointments come, that embitter life in all its after flow. And the main element in all such disappointments can be traced to sin. Pain never stung, sorrow never crushed, disappointment never smote, save as sin gave them power.

And wherein is the power of sin? Only in its being consented to, accepted as a law of life, mode of conduct, or principle of action. It may be intelligently and persistently maintained; it may be only blindly and heedlessly permitted. But if, in fact, it be a law of conduct, as with the unrenewed sinner, then all possibilities of sin come within range and reach of that sinner. Let his own will, prompted by his misconceived interests, counselled by his love of gratification, swayed by his passions, without regard to God's authority or the soul's welfare, be the rule of his conduct; then, at length, in favoring conditions, under press of requisite temptation, any sin he can commit. He is on the way to sins from which he would now shrink with horror. All most horrible crimes, all most damning sins, lie in the way he is going. Perhaps he denies this, and repels it as a slander. It may not seem pertinent to say that he does not know himself; but it is enough to say that he has not wisely read the newspapers.

The restraints of law, the power of social moralities, pride of self-respect, regard for family and friends, sense of safety, ambition for success, the conservative power of good habits, and many like restraints, bar him from crimes, keep him in the ways of good repute, and even lead him in a path which in places runs close by the Christian's. He may even have the part and fairness of Christian guise. But society is daily demonstrating how weak these restraints are; how readily sin can lead a man to break through all such barriers, and plunge into deepest crimes. Frequently the community is shocked by men breaking through all restraints, and letting the sin that inflamed their hearts and festered within, urge them to most horrible crimes. Position in society, domestic relations, self-respect, former habits of morality, voice of conscience, fear of God, and dread of consequences were nothing.

In face of this, all Powers of Evil, certainly the incarnated, insist that sin is a trifle. Were this delusion fully exposed; were the magnitude of sin, the way it works, and the lengths to which it can lead, fully understood and deeply felt, it would raise an alarm, stir fears, lead on to struggles which would give souls deliverence from its power, bring them into the liberty of the gospel, and quickly overthrow the Kingdom of Evil.

But this must not be. All Powers of Evil, from Satan downwards, cry out against it. No such proposition could carry the vote of this world. No such revolution in its affairs will the world permit. Were the Powers of Evil to consent, it would foreclose the "conflict of the ages," bring to ripe maturity the plan which God is leading on to completeness so surely. Alas! so slowly, so slowly, only because the revolution must come, if at all, by consent of individual souls.

To guard against such speedy overthrow; to forestall the ruin which the higher Powers of Evil may know is coming, but which their pride, their unbelief, and their ambition keep concealed even from their own eyes; to put off yet longer the crushing disaster that must come to this rebellion in the final triumph of righteousness; to maintain yet longer at work this vast enginery of sin, — the Powers of the Kingdom of Evil, right here, raise a contest, and dispute the magnitude of sin, the way, certainty, and disaster of its working.

Secretly, they know sin's power, the certainty with which it works, its disaster, and the astounding excesses to which it can go. Secretly, they gloat over its magnitude, and even pride themselves in having so great a venture in hand. But to admit this would be only to invite overthrow. So the magnitude, certainty, disaster, and excesses of sin must be denied at all hazards. All the working forces of the Kingdom of Evil, all apostate spirits of other worlds, all fallen men of this, who have got far enough along to take in the real genius of sin, deny its magnitude, certainty, disaster, and excess.

So we find it. Every sinner is deluding himself

with the conviction that sin is n't much; only a peccadillo; no reason at all for the loss of the soul and its imprisonment in hell. Violation of good manners would trouble them more. If sin shows itself in ome ludicrous shape, they can laugh at it just as heartily as though there was no sin in it. If it brings some immediate pleasure, they accept it as rejoicingly as though there were no damning curse in it. If it yields present ease, and begets carelessness of consequences, they rejoice in freedom from alarm. If a thousand dollars can be made by telling a lie, they ask, What harm is the lie? If a fortune can be made by a life of rascality, who will stop for the rascality? Denial of sin's magnitude, certainty, disaster, and excess, is an element of success in the Kingdom of Evil.

This denial is extensively made, is even characteristic of our times. It not only crops out here and there, but underlies much of our readable literature. Popular writers attribute what of sin they admit to ignorance, bad digestion, malformations, and untoward surroundings; whatever else there is, they regard as a necessary disadvantage of our finiteness. Therefore, so far as it can be cured in this world, their remedies are education, hygiene, social and political reforms, — mere palliatives of sin's curse, but no radical cure of the disease.

Under such narrow and feeble views, the facts of history and the condition of humanity cannot be understood; and, worse still, no right and heroic living is possible. Eliminate the Biblical idea of sin from the mind, and no radical revolution of moral character will transpire; no repentance; no prayerfulness; no earnest conflicts with sin; no alliance of heart with Christ, and no ascent to the level of the heavenly life. All that is likely to be done is a feeble attempt at reform, which will leave the Kingdom of Evil abundant room and success.

CHAPTER V.

PROVINCE CLAIMED BY SIN.

THE Roman Catholic church through much of its history has sought to manage the bestowal and confer the repute of sainthood. Only to martyrs, and such as were eminent in monastic sanctity, has that church given the repute of saintliness, and generally long after their death. The papal church has fashioned the world's convictions in this matter, and modified the current forms of expression. Many call saints only those whom that church has put on the calendar. Here is a somewhat noteworthy fact, that the convictions of the people in the church and out of it, on the subject of sainthood, have been shaped as they would not have been by the ideas and language of the New Testament. Some are called saints without any proof of their saintliness; others not, though believed to be already such before the throne of God.

This is cited in illustration of other things of its sort. It is not the only blunder we have received traditionally. If such blunders are possible, how often may they have been repeated? Without attempting to set any boundary to this field of deceit,

I shall seek to show that there is at least one other in which prevalent convictions are as far from known fact as in the matter of sainthood; namely, a gross traditionary misconception, in the minds both of Christians and sinners, as to the province of religion; whereby it is made to consist in Godward acts of the soul, in devotional exercises and sanctuary services, especially on Sabbath days.

This is fostered by the conscious experience of adult conversions. The prominent thing before the mind of the convert is right adjustment of soul with God. He has found himself a sinner against God, condemned by God's law, in need of God's pardon, and to be saved, if at all, by God's grace. In entering upon the Christian life, his repentance is towards God; at the throne of grace he makes plea for pardon; and the joy that comes is the assurance of the divine favor. What change in human relations this may require is a matter of subsequent, if not secondary, thought.

Indeed, taking the whole history of Christianity, the same general order of thought may be found running through it. The monasticism which marked the early ages of Christian history was a method in which the soul exercised itself in its Godward relations. Retirement to cave or convent was that the soul might lose itself in the rapt meditations of a divinely contemplative spirit. In such seclusion to spend years in holy meditation and in the communion of prayer, was emphatically a religious life. This view of the Christian life, a scholastic monasticism, can be traced in nearly all the centuries of Christian history previous to the Reformation.

In later times, religion, more than before, has gone forth into the world with enlightenment and relief. It has undertaken to reconstruct society. Into marts of trade, with principles of equity; into courts, with principles of enlightened jurisprudence; into the political arena, with the doctrines of justice and freedom; and into halls of legislation, with constitutional law, — Christianity has gone, demanding in all these wider room and freer action for herself, yet in all this never overlooking the fact that the foundation of all betterment in society is the regeneration of individual souls.

Yet there is found, in the church and out, the forenamed fact, a general, perhaps somewhat unexamined impression, that religion is chiefly, if not exclusively, a matter between each soul and God. In looking for confirmation of this statement, it is fitting to leave out all those who have such meagre views of religion as to make it a mere morality, merely a prudent policy for the wise, quiet, and safe ordering of this life. A religion that can do no more; that has no power to restore a fallen soul, not even discrimination to recognize it as a fallen soul; no power to adjust it into lost relations, to revolutionize and inspire it with a higher life than its own, to give it an outlook upon immortality and a use for the universe, — is not a religion worthy of the name, nor of which note is now taken.

As disclosed by God, as illustrated in the life of Christ, and as set forth in writings inspired by the Holy Ghost, also as involved in its essential principles, there is no level of society, no range of life, no place where a right thing can be done, or a wrong, which is not within the province of religion. It refuses restriction within any narrower range. The habitat of religion includes every condition of humanity. Term-time in the school of Christ includes every hour of life. In all places, at all times, something can be accomplished in the religious culture of the soul; for this end there are no wastes, no desert spots in life.

Yet careful inquiry is not at a loss to find Christians who hold the Sabbath as the Lord's, other days their own. Worship in all its forms they count "religious services"; while the services, the activities, that fill up the main bulk of life, are called business, and are thought to be quite devoid of any religious character, — as usually they are. Money given in charity or for religious institutions is held as sacred. The rest is secular. Business, property, and politics lie outside of religion. If, by pressure, religious truth is made to push over into this realm, from some it meets with prompt resent; by others heard respectfully, but with a silent protest and with a determined rejection of the encroachment, — divorcing their business from their religion, in their religion serving God and in business themselves. They are religious occasionally, — in spots.

Were they to study out some intelligent and defensible views in the matter, and write them down for guidance, they would, no doubt, come to very orthodox conclusions, perhaps exhibit a very different life. But this is what few of them ever do; in consequence, they keep a broad line of separation between religion and business. When any interest of the Redeemer's Kingdom comes with claims for service or money, with how many the first instinctive movement of thought and feeling is denial, out of which they must be very carefully persuaded. Something more is needed than a full statement of the case with its warrants of wisdom. Perhaps, for final success, a low and unmanly sentiment has to be appealed to, besides handling their morbid, worldly feelings with great care, and themselves with great consideration.

It is very easy to conceive how differently matters would go if they permitted their religion a wide and free sweep over its legitimate province. Then would they have within the field of their thoughts a contrivance, care, and interest for every welfare of the church and for every aspect of Christ's kingdom. They would be on inquiry to find opportunities for charitable expenditure and Christian investment. All interests of Christ's church at home and of his kingdom abroad would be a part of their business, to be taken into account, planned and provided for. Thus would their lives have a wider sweep, loftier aims, and a healthful spontaneity; and themselves an ennoblement of which they never dreamed.

It is neither slur nor slander to affirm, that in the average conviction of unconverted men, religion is a matter of time and places. They expect to see something of it on the Sabbath, but not on other days; at church, but not on the street; at worship, but not at work. Some utterly deny that it should make any show of itself in politics. They look not for it in business, in the use and control of property, in management of the tongue, in the affinities that have play in social life, in the courtesies that sweeten society, in the silently-done charity, in self-denial for others' good, nor in wrong taken unresentfully. Their blinded minds see religion only at church; and even had they greater spiritual discernment, they might not in many cases find it elsewhere, nor always there.

It were easy to show this to be a gross misconception. Let any one study the character of God, conceive what his moral government involves; let one look at the nature of the soul, at its powers of thought and feeling, its capacity for action, suffering, and enjoyment, its fallen state, what its restoration involves, how truth as a law of life can shape the soul and love transform it; let one see the soul, in the discipline of Christian life, putting forth its powers in a drill of heavenly exercises, fitting for the activities of immortality, playing out influences which, purposely or unconsciously, reflect the image of God and transform other souls into his likeness; let one see that just this enters into all varieties of intelligent Christian life, in all conditions, at all times, on all occasions and in all employment; and religion is readily seen to be, not a thing done, but a life lived, as various as life can be, and as continuous as life must be.

But the aim is not to controvert this conviction, nor inveigh against it, only to consider the fact of its prevalence, in the church and out. Consequences come of it; the most obvious of which, as broad as the fact itself, is that so much of life is shut away from the sphere and reach of religion. Business, travel, pleasure, social life, its affinities and repellancies, domestic life, its principles and spirit, are made to lie outside of the reach and beyond the permitted control of religion.

How it came so, it is difficult to tell. It is not so with some other religions. In India, we find a religion that regulates all smallest particulars of life. Its touch is constant, its power felt every hour. It regulates food and drink, prescribes a code of regulations for social intercourse that are minute and authoritative; in fine, it forbids and commands at every turn in daily life. True, it is a religion of ceremonies, makes slaves of its adherents, leaving no room for the liberty that makes loving sacrifice, trains the soul to no nobility, and gives it neither breadth, volume, nor high aspiration. Yet it makes itself an ever-present power over the soul. Between the Brahminism of India, and Christianity as it lies in the conception of the multitude, this difference is as noteworthy as any: that Brahminism touches the soul of its adherent with a constant power; while Christianity, as so generally misconceived, is a religion of times and places, confined within narrow bounds, leaving long reaches and wide domains of life beyond its permitted sway.

Here the Kingdom of Evil finds another element of success: conceiving that Kingdom merely as including the aggregate of unconverted adults now inhabiting the earth, what have they in hand? Nearly the entire business of the world, something more important, in their esteem, than the churches are ever likely to do. They cannot dispute that Christian men have also a hand in business; the best men in every trade and occupation, yea, sometimes the ruling spirits and controlling power in monetary and commercial centres, and doing well their part in all ramifications of business. But it is worldly business; even Christians count it so, and often draw contrasts between secular employments and religion in a way that leaves the entire realm of business as belonging to the world; and by that they mean the Kingdom of Evil as distinguished from the Kingdom of Christ.

To give the matter a worse look, some Christians conduct business on no higher principles and for no loftier aims than do men of the world. Some drive as hard a bargain, shave as close, and come just as near to downright dishonesty, as can the world's sharpest knave. And when by such, or any means, a fortune has been gathered, the uses some make of it in gratifying pride, in making life luxurious, and in the spendthrift ways of fashionable watering-places, give business a still more worldly aspect.

The talk of men helps the impression that the whole department of business belongs to the Kingdom of Evil. Some of them, even though in the church, disclose a state of mind just as feverishly anxious to get rich as any poor sinner that had no trust in a Heavenly Father. Their hearts go after covetousness; they rejoice over gains and prospects of enrichment just as though there was nothing better in this life. And so the impression gets broadly and deeply made from Monday morning till Saturday night, as all the year's Sabbaths cannot efface, that business is worldliness, with no process of God-serving in it. And worldliness is the Kingdom of Evil. So that Kingdom is made strong by the broad room it occupies.

To make itself still broader and firmer in position, it has claimed for itself exclusive possession of the realm of politics. This, to be sure, has been denied and protested against; men have affirmed that there is a way of doing right and serving God in politics. This is not generally admitted, but strenuously resisted. This matter is not now brought up for dis cussion. It is met with neither admission nor denial; but is held up simply as a fact, maintained by so many, that the province of religion covers not the field of politics.

In this restriction of the province of religion, — shutting it out from the world's business and from its politics; shutting it out also, as could readily be shown, from the whole round of the world's pleasures, — we see the province which Sin arrogates to itself, covering wellnigh the whole field of human activity. Thus we come to see more clearly than before, why this Kingdom of Evil, which at first seemed to have in it only elements of failure, comes to have success, finds room for itself, a magnitude and even dignity that begins to command our respect.

When we come to consider the capital invested, the vast multitude of men employed, their skilled power, their trained minds, their long experience, their capacity of execution, their assiduous application, what invention has found out, how system has arranged all arts, gathered up raw products, adjusted the machinery of manufacture, and established commerce, — all for the realization of our fond product, wealth; when we see, in protecting and fostering all this, that politics, with its tariffs, its banks, its laws, its courts, its diplomacy, and its usages, open all fair and sometimes unfair ways to bring surer and larger wealth; when, too, we see, especially in cities, at fashionable watering-places, and at the National Capitol, how pleasure with her intoxicants urges on the devotees of Mammon to push all economies, industries, and even knaveries, that she may spend with more reckless prodigality, — we see in the Kingdom of Evil very promising elements of success.

If business and politics and pleasure belong exclusively to the Kingdom of Evil, as is claimed by many men, and even conceded by some Christians who keep their religion within such narrow bounds that it has nothing to do save at church and on Sundays, — then, though the Kingdom of Evil be against reason, conscience, and all best powers in man, against all longings and aspirations that ally the soul to God and reach out to immortality, yet that Kingdom of Evil has elements of power and progress which explain its unmerited and otherwise unaccountable success.

CHAPTER VI.

SIN RESPECTABLE IN ITS SHOW.

AS we take into consideration the souls standing under the moral government of God, get any true apprehension of its capacities and inherent necessities, and then look off on its near-by immortality, we readily pronounce the soul's welfare, its religious interests, the most important concern of life. In this respect no one can fail to see, that, by as much as the soul is more than the body, eternity than time, by so much must eternal concerns transcend temporal. Once admit the soul's immortality, its amenability to God, that character here formed settles eternal destiny, and upon these premises one can prove, past all gainsaying, that soul-welfare is the first, foremost, and highest interest of life; that nothing has permanent value, if it fail to help in this; that men living in habitual neglect of the soul, failing to secure its emancipation from sin through God's regenerating grace, and failing to put the soul through a discipline clearly seen to fit it for heavenly society, can be proved fools, in the broadest, most emphatic, and solemn use of that word.

This is a primary truth of religion, and not less of

common-sense. Take the most successful of these men, as the world would measure success; men who have gathered the largest fortunes, surrounded themselves with all ministries of ease and means of enjoyment which cultivated taste could select, or money purchase; or, if their ambition run in a different line, take men who have gained the heights of political life; lay such, suddenly, and in the maturity of life, upon a bed of sickness, from which they know, to their full convincement, the grave is the only escape; and if they accept the plainest facts of religion, they must pronounce their past course the most egregious folly they could commit.

If life is for anything, it is for ends found in immortality. If the education and training of human powers are of any use, the highest of those uses must be in the soul's eternal manhood. The culture of the imagination, the development of reason, the training of thought, the regulation of the temper, the discipline of the heart, the cultivation of the affections, going on to the close of life, must find their highest ranges of use in that life to which this is introductory. Any other conclusion unsettles all our convictions of proportion, fitness, and value.

These are simple doctrines of religion; no less are they profound truths of philosophy. If the soul is for anything worthy of its powers; if God's creations are for any purpose worthy of their magnitude and skill; if the arguments of history are to have any worthy conclusion; if God's moral government is to inaugurate and maintain any state worthy of its principles and processes, or even of the inconceivable myriads of its subjects, — then these consummations must lie further on, in the impending immortality; they are not found in this life.

It becomes, then, the readiest, because a resistless step of logic, that the years of life spent in no intelligent preparation for that immortality, are wasted years. If to occupy life in what is clearly seen to be only a transient interest, be not folly, what is? To occupy powers capable of handling all highest truths and greatest concerns in the universe, to buy these with what in a few years will be nothing,—what language has terms to measure and set forth such folly? This conclusion is resistless. No process of reasoning can overthrow it. It cannot be unsettled or disturbed in the least, except by denials that set everything afloat, that leave no certainties of fact or stabilities of truth on which the soul can rest. We accept the Bible view of life, and its relations to immortality, as the only explanation worthy of our conditions and powers. We see no way of escape from these conclusions, but by denials which throw all things out of connection, and make the world the hopeless ward of an insane asylum. So it seems to us, in the quiet hours of profound meditation.

But when men come to look at this subject from their places of business, themselves clad in the substantial garments of toil, with the zeal of worldliness in their hearts; when their interest in the enterprises of trade and toil is quickened as success requires; when they feel the pressure of accumulated work, the need of enlargement in this direction and that, with the incitement of sure reward and large gains, —

then what a different train of thought will occupy the mind; how close and real and substantial will seem all these enterprises of business! now they have to do with life's foremost and valuable realities; and how dim and distant seem the matters they had in mind during their hours of meditation! The magnitude of business interests give them a respectability and consideration which the Kingdom of Evil assumes to itself and makes an element of success.

The argument assumes, for its fullest presentation, an enumeration, a summing-up of all business values. But this would lead to figures beyond definite comprehension. The misconception that puts all business beyond the province of religion, puts all the capital invested in farms, town and city lots, buildings, manufactories, railroads, steamers, ships of commerce, merchandise, securities, and banking, into the use of the Kingdom of Evil, as belonging to it. Under this false yet general view, let one stand where he can have a bird's-eye view of the world's business, as seen in a Western grain and lumber emporium, and note the impression it makes on his mind; let him see the rush and hear the roar of teams, carting in and out, as commerce demands; look down upon long ranges of deep and high warehouses, filled with products of all climes; steamers, propellers, and other craft sailing out and into the harbor, freighted with wealth; a thousand cars arriving daily, some from Atlantic, some from Pacific coast; others departing to such far-off destination, all freighted with produce and merchandise, whose value utterly bewilders the mind. Following these streams of wealth as they sweep eastward to some commercial emporium, let him see them dashing, like maddened waters upon counter streams, as they sweep in from foreign lands, the one to find way to places of home consumption, the other to ports across the ocean.

Then, from such a general observation, let him go down and stand for an hour in some wholesale house, and see the amount and value of goods daily received and sold; or at the counter of some bank, and note the average of exchanges between paying and receiving tellers; and then remember that all along these streets are miles of such wholesale and banking houses, and he will have a confused and bewildered idea of the immense quantities and vast capital occupied in the world's business. Business summing up such vast aggregates, handling such heavy capital, occupying so many hands and best trained minds in the country, even if it is all outside religion, as is claimed by many and conceded by some, nevertheless commands respect for its intricacy and gigantic proportions.

And the men engaged in it feel that they are doing the real business of this world and this life. To them what the world is for is to have such things done. The world emerged from its old geologic ages and keeps swinging along its orbit for just this use. The years come that they may be filled with such transactions. Using time, money, and all powers of mind in such occupations, men feel that they are putting things to their right use, and filling out for themselves a life fullest orbed. This view gets impressed on the minds of men who have higher and broader views, but who cannot resist the dominant spirit of the age.*

We may argue against it; deny that religion is shut up in such narrow province; affirm that its sphere reaches wherever right things can be done, or wrong; that all business is to be only a method of God-serving; that it is to be undertaken and prosecuted on such principles, in such a spirit, and with such aims, that it shall consciously be a religion, confirming the soul in Christian obedience, dignifying life, and refreshing the heart as would a season of worship. But the extent to which we hear Christians complain of the untoward influence of business on their religion, the divorce and antagonism in which they are held, show how largely they have failed to accept business as a sphere of religion. And so all the respectability that comes from the vast aggregate and heavy capital of the world's business, is put to the credit of the Kingdom of Evil. In such service a man feels that he is making something of himself; that herein he finds his true worth and dig-

* In illustration, a clergyman called on his parishioner, by previous arrangement, for his donation to an important fund. Finding him engaged in business, he apologized for his intrusion and offered to withdraw, just as though it was any intrusion to come, by previous appointment, into a Christian man's office, on business pertaining to the advancement of the Redeemer's Kingdom. The parishioner accepted the courtesy as befitting the dignity of wealth, and presented his check for a large amount. We are concerned only in the air of the thing, the understanding, the felt conviction, which forced itself upon men who knew better, that religion must come to business in very humble attitude, and, like a poor relation, offer apology for the trusion.

nity. It sometimes troubles him, that his is a life of sin; but religion is so distant, shut up in such narrow province of mere worship, so indefinite as compared with the palpable realities of business, that the latter, to the exclusion of religion, gains his thoughts, absorbs his heart, and incorporates his life into the Kingdom of Evil. The readily seen and appreciated substantialness of business, its vast amounts and consequent respectability, help that Kingdom to success.

Take another of the world's great concerns, — war. What splendors attach to the movement of an army, the encampment, a review of troops, the evolutions of artillery, the march to battle, the grandeur of the conflict, and the exultation in victory. Any sight of these leaves it no matter of wonder that so much glory attaches to military life. When we read graphic accounts — knowing them to be tame beside the reality — of battles that gave this nation union, freedom, and peace, we feel to have had part in so great a struggle was to make those years of life memorable. War prosecuted in defence of national life and solidarity has abundant justifications. Upon it God's blessing has been invoked and bestowed. Yet what guilt is theirs who stir up the strifes of war. Take any war, a campaign, or even a single battle, Gettysburg or Sedan; see the loss of life, sufferings of the wounded, the grief that comes to so many homes, to stay so long; and none can doubt the guilt of those who "let slip the dogs of war."

Yet, without question of its justification, always readily found, to have had part in war, to have shown bravery, to have won battles, to have risen to command, to have become the proud commander of an army, — how much more is this, in common estimation, than to have become a truly Christian man? to be called a general or commodore, than simply a Christian brother? War for aggression, conquest, or oppression clearly belongs to the Kingdom of Evil. Yet when there attaches to war all the guilt that can, how magnificent an affair it still can be! How intoxicating the power it puts on man! How exciting its chances! With what absorbing interest its campaigns unfold! To have had part in these, to have been in high command, how much more is thus offered to many, than all that can be found in the whole round of a religious life and its eternal issues!

So take politics. We admit the possibility and the rare fact, that one can be a political man for ends that are pre-eminently right and Christian. Of such, instances can be found that match any patriotism or heroism in the world's history. On the political arena, our own country and others are not wanting in noble specimens of humanity. But take political life in its more frequent aspect, where each man's endeavor is determined chiefly and obviously by personal ambition,— the party and its principles succeeding as well under another's leadership,— take just that run of politics which belongs to the Kingdom of Evil, whose personal ambition is stimulated by popularity, office, salary, power, and perquisites, how exciting and alluring the chances opened to ambition! For success, what will not be endured? To gain the high ends of ambition, to have office and power, how much more real, substantial, and satisfactory than anything religion can offer, — to go to Congress worthier of effort than to go to heaven!

Glance at one thing more,— pleasure; and at only one of its many scenes. For pleasure and gayety a man takes his family to a fashionable watering-place. He may rent a cottage for $1,000 to $5,000. Variations of dress, style of carriage and team, attendance of servants, mode of living, and round of dissipation must correspond. So at an expense of $10,000 or more, a few months of pleasure come and go with all their variations, excitements, and intoxicating delights. The ride, the sail, the surf-bathing, the gossip with newly-arrived friends, the flutter of new fashions, the evening party, the dance, perhaps gambling also; put to no necessity of counting cost, how intoxicating a few such weeks to lovers of pleasure! How many rush to such places that they may have company with the gay spendthrifts of what is called "fashionable life"! To how many this is more than religion can offer!

To be rich, or to be Christian; to have high command in military life, or to be Christian; to have office and power in politics, or to be Christian; to have the luxury of pleasure at Saratoga, Nahant, or Long Branch, or to be Christian: put to the choice of only one, how many would choose something else than to be Christians? So the Kingdom of Evil, by its own claims, partly by consent of those who know better, has taken possession of business, war, politics, and pleasure, — made these great concerns of worldliness so attractive, so respectable, given them such dignity, and thus sway, over the minds of men, that they are grand elements of success in the Kingdom of Evil.

CHAPTER VII.

CONCEALMENTS OF SIN.

THINGS look differently from different points of observation. It is so with a landscape, conduct, and the whole drift of historical events. The Northern aspect and the Southern of our late war were very different. From one point of vision the wonder is that the Kingdom of Evil finds any success. It is so at variance with highest welfare in the long run; so peremptorily forbids a man to make the most of himself; throws him out of adjustment with God and the universe; makes so little of his powers and opportunities; puts him into such disturbances and discords; embroils him in so many difficulties; can awaken such terrible fears; fret him with so many exasperations, and in the end brings him to such remediless ruin, — that, judging simply from the nature of the case, one would think that the Kingdom of Evil, at the beginning, and all through its history, would have dragged, fallen behind, and never come to any respectable success. It has all elements of failure, as seen in one aspect; and if in the history of any soul, or world, the Kingdom of Evil had proved an utter abortion, very good reasons could have been given.

Looking at it from another point of vision makes quite a difference. Let the sense of immortality be deadened, as with so many, so that, though a hereafter of conscious existence be held theoretically, there shall practically, day after day, be maintained an utter forgetfulness of the proximity and certainty of the grand events coming; also, in face of all the terrible things it is doing, let sin be counted a trifle, the difference between Christian and sinner denied; let religion be shut up to the narrow province of religious observances and sacred times, leaving the attractive and frequented spaces of life aloof from its claim and power; let sin be made respectable in the attractive show it makes in business, war, politics, and pleasure, and reasons begin to appear why the Kingdom of Evil may have success. This is further explained by the fact that guilt is concealed by the attractiveness and profit of sin.

The moral repugnance of sin is concealed by the attractions thrown around it. On popular streets in cities and at fashionable watering-places are opened drinking and gambling houses. One whose idea of such places is formed by what is found where society is only dead enough to ferment moderate corruption, can have no conception of the attractive gorgeousness in which sin can be arrayed. Looking at such a temple of vice, even as seen from the street, noting the grandeur of its architectural proportions, its richness of adornment, its palatial rooms and luxurious furniture, — seen through the glass frontage, it might seem a fit abode of angels, rather than demons. While, in view of their use, they are fitly called "gambling hells," they might, in view of their structure and adornment, not inappropriately be called gambling heavens.

Not only is there ready supply for every appetite and passion, something to meet and delight every sense, but let the senses, by long indulgence, become preternaturally delicate and quick to detect and enjoy all nicest shades of quality in gourmandism, and there is supply for any appetite, however capricious or expensive. If one prides himself in being a connoisseur in liquids, and demands, at fabulous cost, wines brought from far and preserved through long years, his appetite can be gratified; that in this his pretence of palate-skill is met by pretence as to the origin and age of the wines furnished, only shows what an equal match shams can make.

Not only every sense of the body, but powers of mind, are met with gratification. Does a cultivated taste demand superbly furnished apartments, adorned with costly works of art, multiplied by massive mirrors? All this can be found in rooms luxuriously furnished, magnificently draped, brilliantly lighted, and supplied with costly paintings, statuary, and other artistic ministries of delight. Seldom has refined taste, inspired by love of family and home, with wealth at command, been able to gather into any princely residence appliances for gratification, ministries to ease, and instruments of delight, found in some of these temples of vice and ruin.

The managers of these establishments, though brutal when necessary, can show an easy and courtly politeness. They are men of intelligence, travel, and wide social range. They know the ways of the world, can meet highest classes on their own level, and prove agreeable company to any most cultivated. And even the waiters show an obsequiousness which leads a man, capable of such inflation, to feel himself on a higher level than he had supposed within his reach. If a man could meet the bills, could quiet conscience, hush all voices of reason, stifle all longing for the greater things of which the soul is capable, if he could only forget God, immortality, and all grand realities of life, how pleasant to while away an evening, and many of them, in such an establishment! How beautiful sin can be! How entirely can its attractions conceal its guilt and danger!

In such establishments, by their polite and courtly managers, men are made drunkards, gambled out of their fortunes, and then turned out of those palaces of luxury, elegance, and adornment, some insane with drunkenness, others crazed by loss of fortune, and often ready for suicide. Such ruin comes every week to some. Fondest hopes, brightest prospects, noblest powers, and grand possibilities are smitten down, elegantly to be sure, but swiftly and with fell certainty. This ruin, once wrought, sweeps away in underground channels seldom seen by the public eye. That fair temple of vice and ruin stands as alluring and tempting to coming victims, as it did to those who have been sacrificed and are gone. Its embellishments conceal, perhaps adorn, the sins they are made to serve. How beautiful and bewitching, enshrined in what glories so ruthless, a sin as gambling can be. With such helps the Kingdom of Evil must have some success.

For like end, but by different methods, the same thing is done in the theatre. Higher powers of mind are appealed to and lower passions. The adornments of the theatre are more flashy and tawdry; but in the histrionic art, addressing itself, as it can, to some of the noblest powers of the mind, the charm of stage scenery, the brilliancy of the assembly, the lights, the gayety and music, the central attraction and accompaniments, give the theatre a fascination over varied classes of mind. Those who cannot be won by severe exhibitions of the histrionic art in its higher ranges, can be drawn by the buffoonery of the comedy, ballet-dancing, and by what more there is further on and lower down, stirring the vilest sensualities, with near-by opportunities of gratification. O, how brilliant and gay vice can be! And, too, so near at hand, indulgences for every lust that burns, and every passion that rages in corrupt humanity! All these are presented with an air of respectability, with attractions and an outside look of decency that hide the sin and give it success.

By still another method the same thing is done in the ball-room, where the comparatively pure submit to a handling they would instinctively resent outside of the dance; where delicacy loses its bloom; and what lies further on, beyond that, it would be sad to say or even think. This sin of "lovers of pleasure more than lovers of God" is concealed by the festivity of the scene, the flash of lights, the attraction of company, the gayety of the music, and the splendor of attire. As a marked instance of the latter, the newspapers report that a lady at Washington lately promenaded in a ball-room, bearing upon her person clothing and ornaments valued at $75,000. Embellished in what adornments pride can be! How gay extravagance can appear! What attracting guise vanity can put on!

Sin is the original cause of all disaster in the universe, of all discord among nations, of all wretchedness in families, and of all ruin to souls. It can even send its desolations down upon the materialities of nature. Such is its drift and power; but to those who cannot see this, so at war is it to every sense of welfare and security, so opposed to man's best powers in their noblest ranges of action, that one would think sin, by its own nature, barred the way to success. But when we see how it is concealed by the attractions thrown around it, how fascinating its guise, how captivating its indulgences, and how respectable its practice, we find there are reasons for its unmerited success.

So, again, sin is concealed under the cover of its immediate profit. Why, there are men who, for one fair snatch at the wealth that lady bore along in her promenade through a Washington ball-room, — for one fair snatch with both hands, — would be willing she should immediately sink through the grave to hell. How small are the sums, as told in the newspapers and proved in court, which can blind a man to the guilt of murder, and hide from the perpetrator all sense of its magnitude. A few dollars have done that.

What is a lie, — a lie as plain, positive, emphatic, and well constructed as a lie could be, — in comparison with some small profit? How, in the esteem of many, is its guilt concealed by a cent more per yard, per pound, per bushel; by a dime more per ton, or a dollar more per acre? Some would not entertain the question for a moment, but would tell the lie with the quickness and ease of instinct.

A drinking and billiard saloon is opened. No very great fortune can be made at it, — not more than in some useful handicraft. For the sake of profit so small, a man will be willing to imperil the morals of youth and men with gray hairs, seducing them to laziness, gambling, and intemperance. He lives in an atmosphere of low thought, breathes vulgarity and consents to it, partly because he never conceived that the world had anything purer. To his vision sin is concealed, its profits hide its enormity from his sight; and to his mind it is the least conceivable objection to any act or course, to say it is wrong.

On that memorable Friday, when gold ran up to such giddy heights in New York, and gambling in gold raged with such maniacal force, the newspapers say a western man telegraphed his broker in Wall Street to buy him gold to a certain amount, which was done. Later he telegraphed his broker to sell and remit the proceeds. The gain was $28,000. With that sum before his eyes, how could he see the guilt of gambling? Many on that day, able to issue such orders, put their property in peril, as did that western man, and lost, losing large fortunes and turning themselves out of valuable homesteads. And many, unable to issue such orders, wished they had the power. Speedy gains concealed the guilt of gambling, and all that side of desolatian and ruin which lies opposite to its gains, brought by luck as modified by skill of knavery. Forgetting its false principles, its lack of legitimate productiveness, its side of loss and ruin, and looking only at some notable instance of gain, how many let its speedy gains hide entirely its guilt.

Even where there is a professed conformity to the legitimate principles of business, the respectability of sin hides the wrong it may come handy to commit. Defrauding creditors, failing rich, where the rascality is so neatly done that officers of the law find no chance to rip up the fraud, a cheating in which the ingenuity or covetousness outwits all the wisdom of legislation, — how often thus the gain and the sharpness of the trickery conceal the guilt from the eyes of the actors, and even from others who should have clearer vision.

The use of third parties as innocent purchasers, lack of legal proof by deft concealment, limitations of time taken advantage of, and other weak points which show our laws to be of human origin, have been the turning-points of amassment and success in the history of many a fortune. And the large gains thus made sure, while without the security and honor of honestly-gained wealth, hide from the possessors the guilt which should make them uneasy in their gains. The stain of guilt is on many a fortune; but what care the owners if the respectability and power of their possessions enable them to carry themselves bravely before men? For present power and position conscience can be hushed, human rebuke and even eternal retributions can be braved.

Sin is concealed, too, by the insignificance of the acts in which it is sometimes illustrated. When the cheat amounts only to a few cents; when the wrong works damage to some insignificant personage; when the lie wrought only an inconvenience; when failure in the contract brought only small loss; when the uncharitableness involved only temporary suffering; the sin is hidden by the insignificance of the results. To have care for such peccadilloes seems like holding conscience under bonds of fastidiousness.

There is no fixed zero point, as with thermometers. It is a sliding-scale. Every sin seems small, if only a little larger than one usually commits, even when his ordinary sins are crimes at which most would shudder. With slight uneasiness, some commit sins that would sorely wound the conscience of others. The murderous blow that enables the robber to carry out his plans is so slight a departure from his ordinary conduct that it gives him no uneasiness. Habit and familiarity help in the same line. A long indulged sin has all thought of guilt dropped out of it. Only when it works some unusual disturbance, or brings some unwonted damage, will its character as sin arrest the notice of the perpetrator. So, even, the natural laws of mental action help to hide sin, and give the Kingdom of Evil success.

Sin is concealed by not being seen in its perfected fruit, only in its flower. The full harvest of woe is not seen in its beauteous flower. The murderer saw no guilt of blood in the lust of gain he nourished. He was intoxicated with the power of wealth. For its increase he was barred by no knavery, and so the way was opened for the guilt of blood, no sight of which did he see in his early-nursed passion for gain. What drunkenness does a young man see in his pleasant tippling? By the way he is entering others have gone; he is enchanted with the festivities that led them to ruin. The hilarious gayety of companionable drinking is all he can see. He has not gone far enough in corrupting his physical system with the disease of drunkenness to find in his bodily condition any urgent call for intoxicants. He is in pursuit only of merriment, and cares only to meet the misconceived demands of social festivity; so he sees not the woes of intemperance and its kindred vices that lie further on. Even when he has gone further and finds in his physical state reason for a resort to the cup, a little easement of disagreeable sensations is all that he looks for. He sees only the flower. What time will bring, what lies further on, — the wretchedness and ruin of drunkenness,—are totally concealed from his sight. All the ways that grow so devious and end at last in vice and crime, verge off from the path of rectitude by such imperceptible degrees, that the divergence is not detected. Ordinary forecast takes in no such distant results. But there is a crowding in that direction; the movement may be unsteady and irregular; it may be terribly swift; but if no retractive movement be begun, the end will be reached and found to be ruin.

Concealment of sin is an element of success in the Kingdom of Evil. To the subjects of that Kingdom the horizon of life shuts down close by; the results of conduct, lying beyond the boundary of this life, appear little to them, less controlling over conduct than the weather, of less importance than the business of to-morrow. Business that exceeds not five dollars per day, pleasures that might not be thought possible of engaging the thoughts of any above the age of childhood, conceal, day after day, through years, the central realities and verities of life. These verities are not the considerations by which their plans are shaped, in which their powers find stimulus, by which feelings are regulated and all convictions modified. In concealment from these verities sin works and so finds success.

And yet this concealment is no easy matter. Society in all its forms of organization seems as if constructed on purpose to keep sin from dropping out of notice. It is a force working in society, against which, on all sides, men must defend themselves by a constant warfare. Nevertheless, sin works in concealment; is counted a trifle by how many otherwise intelligent men; is hidden by the adornments wherewith it is garnished by its immediate profits, by the petty acts in which it is illustrated, the homœopathic doses in which it is offered; by being seen in incipient growths and not in full fruitage; and by the respectability of its success.

And this is a fruitful element of success in the Kingdom of Evil. Sin kept in concealment, counted only a trifle, who will hold it the central object and highest aim of life to make war against a hidden trifle? Who will shape his plans and adjust himself to the discipline of life, to work himself free from sin's power? And who will raise any earnest cry to God for deliverance? So sin comes to be a controlling power in many a business, an impulse in many a heart, a crystallizing force in many a family, and a dominant spirit in society.

CHAPTER VIII.

SPIRITUAL INDISCRIMINATION.

MOST persons are puzzled in trying to conceive the experience of a royal personage, as Queen Victoria. There is a difference in queens, as seen in contrasting the reigning Queen of England and the exiled Queen of Spain. But take such a queen as Victoria, one who has failed in no function of queenhood, how different her outlook upon life from that of her average subjects! Beneath her is a political and social order, both vast and intricate, in all its layers and relations so adjusted and constructed that she may be its head, a kingdom that she may wear a crown.

It would bother one to enumerate even in thought all the materials and constituent parts of a nation; but all these, to remotest colony and humblest official, have reference to her. Born to such an inheritance; coming into peaceable possession of it while in the bloom of maidenhood; taking for her help the husband of her choice; holding unquestioned possession of her throne for a long life-time, and expecting to leave it as the undisputed possession of her descendants, — here is a life, in outward conditions, as wide as possible from the average of her subjects.

Yet, when we tear off the outward husk, forget the external show, conditions, and circumstances ot her life, and come to the inward reality of personal history, we find the commonness of human experience standing out in marked prominence. As a maiden, woman, wife, mother, and widow, Queen Victoria has thoughts, convictions, emotions, longings, fears, anxieties, hopes, sorrows, and rejoicings, common to every other maiden, woman, wife, mother, and widow, tinged to some different color, shaped to some different form, yet the same substantially.

So in the less marked extremes found in this country, the man who combines in his own person and condition greatest wealth, broadest views, richest culture, and most generous spirit, contrasted with some poorest, narrowest, and ignorantest man, — the differences strike the mind first, and are all that some can see. They are prominent and palpable, showing themselves in habitation, dress, manners, gait, occupation, in style of language, range of thought, and in every exhibition which the two make of themselves every hour of the day. Even exchange of home and dress could not hide the most marked differences.

Passing from the outward and looking at the inward experience of these two men, the differences begin to fade away and their similarities become more prominent. Hunger and cold pinch each. The refreshment of sleep comes as gratefully to the one as to the other. Success and failure help and hinder each alike. To each the truths of mathematics and morals speak the same language. Conscience speaks in the same tones. The kindness of love, the inspiration of hope, the depressment of fear, the pressure of anxiety, and the weight of sorrow lay equal hand on both. Each finds difficulties as hard to surmount, life's struggles as full of strains. Taking the substantial contents of their lives, what is offered to them through the senses, what is done by the involuntary action of the mind, by impulse of social feeling, the similarities of human nature overcount the differences; and despite the latter we say: "A man 's a man for a' that."

Where this doctrine of man's wholeness prevails, civil law helps to keep the essential similarity in view. In some States it took a man and $250 to vote; ordinarily, a man can do it without help of property, and, since the adoption of the Fifteenth Amendment, without any question as to complexion. So, if a man is murdered, the law does not stop to inquire whether he was rich or poor, learned or ignorant, white or black. It is enough that he was a man. Or, if one be guilty of crime, his station in life, his natural gifts, his acquired powers, or his neglect to make more of himself, avail nothing in a court of justice. "Equality before the law" gives each his chance. The chief things in this equality are the divine bestowments, as in essential powers of body and mind, materials necessary to living, conditions for activity, a fair chance at life's work; in what men are made to be originally, and in what is offered to their acceptance, are found their main similarities. From this somewhat varied, yet common level, they start.

When, now, we come to turn this whole matter

round and look at it on the other side, when we come to see how men have modified their original powers, how they have taken what was offered them through nature and society, the uses to which they have put themselves, their opportunities and surroundings; then their similarities begin to fade away; prominent characteristics and differences come into view. Even the civil law, which tried to hold all men to an equality in its presence, begins to esteem and handle them very differently. Some it lets go free through life, choosing their own abode, occupation, and associates, careful only to protect them in their enjoyment of essential rights. Others it suddenly arrests in their enjoyments and pursuits, calls them to account, puts them under bonds, amerces them, or hurries them off to prison, there to stay for years, perhaps for life; and the law counts itself competent to hurry a man out of life by a sudden and violent death.

But where this may not be, whatever the convicted murderer's desire to walk forth on the broad earth among men, to breathe the free air of heaven and look up into its star-lit dome; however restless his craving to put body and mind into the work and struggle of life; however earnest his longing to keep himself in the affinities and attractions of social life, and in the endearment of domestic relations,—he must enter into that dungeon where he may hear the roar of life around him, but from which he may never come forth, till Death turns jailer. Those powers of body and mind which made him ache for the struggle and toil of life, must lie in rusting disuse, sinking to idiocy or fretting themselves into insanity; those impulses of social and domestic life must be denied all manifestation and reciprocity, till the heart shall become as dead and cold as the idiotic mind, or as frenzied as the maniac's. Even the civil law counts itself justified in giving men such treatment.

Although social life cannot go to such extremes, it is even more critical in detecting differences among men, and has more emphatic ways of pronouncing its convictions. Society throws up invisible yet formidable barriers which certain may not pass. Families in the same neighborhood have as little to do with each other as if separated by a Babel-confusion of tongues; though living on the same street, yet as far separated as intervening miles could make them: "So near and yet so far." Where society has become intensely organized, large expenditures have been made and much snubbing endured in the attempt to gain a higher grade of social life. The attempt of the suddenly rich to pass themselves into circles of better culture, and the rebuff they meet upon exposure of their uncouth manners, their bad grammar, and stolid ignorance, have formed ready themes for wit and ridicule.

Passing the artificial distinctions which wealth builds up, more substantial laws of separation are found. One of these is diversity of culture. There are men whose range of thought is so much above another's that they have little in common, scarcely touch beyond the theme of weather. What works equally well in maintaining separations is a jealous sensitiveness, fearing any exposure of thought or sentiment, lest it should betray ignorance or weakness, and so wound self-vanity. Suspicion works separation. One sees some betterment of condition or culture in others, and in his lack of magnanimity thinks such better men have the same supercilious pride he would feel, and so holds himself aloof, as if contact would bring him under contempt of this imaginary pride.

Passing all separations coming from diversity of natural powers, education, position, and from the use one has made of outward opportunities and social surroundings, we come upon the deepest and broadest differences; and these are found in moral character. Here are differences which even the civil law recognizes and can measure with its coarse instruments. It aims to sift out from among the people all lawless and criminal men. All differences, even the greatest, it cannot notice. It arrests and brings to punishment only men convicted of moral turpitude as violators of civil law.

The characteristic qualities of manhood come not from outward condition, not from surroundings nor from original gifts. For moral character is the highest and most definitive quality of manhood. "Not that which enters into a man defileth," or ennobleth him. Not gifts of natural endowment, not original powers, genius, position, inheritance, or bestowment; not what is offered to him, but what comes from him; not what he takes, but what he gives, determines his moral character. It is manufactured in him, and is known only as he gives it out.

This process of manufacture is constantly going on. One takes certain definite laws of conduct, as to enjoy himself, to do as he pleases, to act as present interest or impulse requires, or as is most accordant with the spirit and tone of surrounding society; another takes, as principles of conduct, the law of God, the law of right, the law of love. One has certain aims, as, to enjoy life, to increase his wealth, to gratify his ambition; another has, as his aim, to secure God's favor and renewing grace, and thus the salvation of his soul. One walks after the flesh; another after the spirit. One lives wholly for what is in this world; another for the grand things of immortality. One separates his soul from God; another allies his soul to God. And so the cardinal distinction of sinner and Christian arises, running its line of demarcation through society, to spiritual discernment the greatest difference among men.

Here are two sorts. There are more. Not more varied are human faces than human souls. Souls are as varied as are human condition, experience, and the ways these are taken; for these fashion souls. On the same level and even in the same family condition varies, and experience more, since it is varied by the way condition is taken. No parent can train any two children exactly alike. Shades of temperament, tones of disposition, require different handling. And what is alike in treatment is taken in a different way, and so brings a varied product of character; no two alike, more than foregone and fashioned experience.

The same thing is repeated in adult life. Here condition varies even more than in childhood. If seemingly, in general, the same, it is made different by variety of disposition. Thus condition, to all appearance the same, contents one and frets another, making that similar condition very dissimilar. Temperament, disposition, health, connections, pressure and direction of ambition, one's tact and culture, make conditions of life different, even if before they had been adjusted to nicest similarity. Even in conditions so alike as to afford no discoverable difference, some most fortuitous circumstance, a casual remark, some impression of nature, or any most trifling event may turn the stream of life in one direction or another, settle it into some rut of habit, making life and soul a changed product. Turning thus from condition to the way it is taken, to each one's action, responsive to truth, providence, reason, conscience, surroundings, and associations, considering all that is comprised in experience, we find causes of diversity adequate to account for all differences; even if it be proved that, with souls as with faces, there is only one of a sort.

The differences among men, and especially those pertaining to moral character, are not found simply by the curious and inquisitive. The action of society brings them out. Every man is constantly publishing himself. Even if he be secretive, he must publish that fact. The attractions of life lead men to betray themselves; and when these fail, its frictions wear off the varnish and show the grain of a man's disposition. And so comes the humiliating fact, that men generally are better understood than they suppose. This holds true of all nicest shades of difference, and much more, of that greatest difference found between Christian and sinner, whenever acquaintance discloses character.

Many are blind in discerning character, giving the theme no study. Then, too, sinful and Christian characters in this life are in a embryotic state, yet to come to mature development; still, even under these difficulties, their differences stands out prominently in the convictions of discerning men. This is the most marked separation running through society. And it would seem as if God had ordered all the conditions and appointments of life so as to keep it perpetually in sight. Each man is compelled habitually to run to the court of conscience with points for adjudication, and then afford illustration. Perpetually, as time comes, comes the question, how to use it. The strong enginery of life will not let a man stand still; yet he cannot stir without giving shape or confirmation to moral character. Wants press him to a perpetual doing, and that involves a constant drill in moralities. Men are brought into such relations of business, into such affinities of friendship, into such ties of domestic life, that to be is to do, and to do is to give character nearer perfection in sin or holiness. Competition in business, contest in rivalship, conflict of interests, which bring such a close set-to of struggle, put character into shape and show, this or that, sinful or Christian. No day goes by, hardly an hour, in which demonstrations are not made, visible to each one's consciousness, and more visible to others than is comfortable to self-respect.

In consequence, here and there, in beautiful consistency and with cheering light, shines the grace of humility, or resignation, or peace, charity, purity, the heavenly-mindedness of genuine sainthood, in all sorts of homes, from highest to humblest. Here and there can be seen inflexibility of principle, bravery of faith, dignity of Christian balance, — all these amid provocations that fret and craze others out of their proprieties.

And then sin, not to be behind in anything, must publish itself, even if thereby it publish its shame, according to God's everlasting decree. Its shame is too common, its sounds too familiar to need description. The world is full of it. It would seem that pride, if not manly self-respect, would lead the sinner to be more modest with his attainments. But in the level where he stands, in the associates he gathers, in the assemblages to which he resorts, in the spirit he indulges, and in the bearing he carries towards others, he is putting into conspicuousness the sinfulness, and not less the shame, of his character. The ordinary appointments of life marshal men out into segregation. Who go to the sanctuary, and who to the saloon; who to the prayer-meeting and who to the gaming hall; who worship on the Sabbath, and who ride out for pleasure; who find recreation in the sanctities of home, and who among the promiscuous characters in a public ball-room, — these are well understood. Society is very frank with her disclosures. Men have hardly pride enough to win self-respect. Then there is always some great question on hand, half moral, half political, or purely moral; or some great enterprise of progress, here and there touching the welfare of society, helping to establish truth, or give the gospel wider sweep; and these questions no sooner get to the heat of debate, than men arrange themselves on this side or that, as if on purpose to announce their moral characters.

Now, in the face of all these distinctions, differences so broad, visible, and palpable, shown up in such variety, placed in such wide separation, and held up so persistently to the gaze of all men, the Kingdom of Evil, in its very genius and spirit, by varied and constant inculcation, is producing in the minds of its subjects the conviction, that all men stand about on a level, — some better in some respects, others in others; that all have about an equally fair chance and about equal success; they are on different levels, have different aims, but get along equally well — for them; all in the same boat, and may expect, at last, like treatment and compassion from the same pitying God.

This is the indiscriminating generality of a lazy universalism. No breadth of view, no keen insight, no deep convictions; but a shiftless, shirking generalization, that overlooks all differences and lumps all sorts together. Having the free air in common, partaking of nature's bounties together, having like wants, powers, and impulses, these men of generalities take such outward and material facts of condition to foretoken like treatment all the way through. They forget that moral government has to do with moral character; and that moral character comes not from what is offered to man, but from the way he takes it, from the response he makes to all God's disclosures and dealings.

This element of power and prevalence in the Kingdom of Evil is not at all, or at least less, a conviction affirmed by reason and sanctioned by conscience, than a vague impression, an unsifted feeling, that refuses to be confronted by truth, or to give itself into the handling of argument. And just for this reason it has greater power and sway. It prevails with that large class, the heedless, men who feel safe enough, resting on a guess that matters will come out right in the end.

Let this conviction, or, if it have not warrant enough to be a conviction, this feeling have sway, and how easy matters will go. Some care may be necessary to keep from conflict with the civil law, to preserve reputation and good standing in society; but, aside from this, what a free-and-easy life a man can live. No severe discipline, no struggles for betterment, no war against impulses, no restraint upon appetite, no bridle on the tongue, no crucifixion of lusts, no longings for a higher life, no prayer for deliverance, no attempt at rescue, backed up by conflicts and crowned with victories; hardly a heedless concern for present or future. Under such regimen, how surely will a man run down; how safely included in the Kingdom of Evil. He stands in a bog that has no reactive ground from which he can begin ascent.

The Kingdom of Evil is so much a success, up and down the ages and the world over, because in the minds of indiscriminating men the feeling prevails that all are about alike, and may expect like treatment from the All-Merciful. This feeling is in opposition to what is most visible and multiplied in society. It disintegrates moral government and character, and fuses all convictions into a blind guess. Yet men let that feeling have sway. It fashions their lives, keeps them aloof from all struggles for salvation, and proves itself an essential and prolific element of success in the Kingdom of Evil.

Sin, taken in all its length and breadth, in its height and depth, in its history and results, is the most stupendous cheat with which the human mind ever had to do. Taking up either its principles or projects, its methods or results, it would seem an easy task for reason to prove, that from the start it should be a failure, as it will be in the long run; since what is eternally and infinitely fit will become real. But the end is not yet. So, against all antecedent probabilities, seemingly certainties of failure, the Kingdom of Evil has come to respectable success, at least in this world; not in some eras or countries, but the world over, and through all history. And this fact, though without justifications, is not without reasons.

CHAPTER IX.

PERVERTED MENTAL ACTION.

UPON the ocean, on the land, on hill-top and valley, field and forest, wherever the light shines, every ray is true to the law of its motion. Light and shade, shine and shadow, everywhere present themselves just as the laws of light require. If conditions of refraction exist, the rays are refracted without any stubbornness or exception. In its reflection every ray is mathematically exact. Angles of incidence and reflection preserve their equality in all cases, even if infinite in number. If conditions of polarization exist, then light is polarized. Light asks for no humoring, has no waywardness to be overcome by persuasion; over longest distances there is no lagging behind; unwatched, it follows its law, as if under the gaze of a thousand philosophers. Into eyes of beast, bird, and insect it photographs pictures with the same exquisite perfection as into human eyes. And it serves the eyes of ignorantest men with the same care and nicety as if they had given years to studying the laws of light.

So, taking any other power in nature, it would be found to prove itself true to the law of its action in all cases. From the growth of tiniest plant to the motion of a planet wheeling round the sun, nowhere a blunder. Diseased action there is, because disease has come to be one of the forces of nature which has its law of action; and these, unarrested, it follows with fell certainty. But refusal is nowhere found in the realm of nature; amid all her voices there is not heard — "I won't."

When, however, we come up to the level of moral beings, we begin to hear dissent uttered in emphatic tones. And the rebellion, here started, is so great a disturbance that it must carry damage into all its surroundings. It mars what might be thought remote from its influence, as seen in the wreck indulgence of passion brings to the body. Much more would we expect it to mar what is nearer, the mental powers. Comparatively few minds, even under the discipline of education and the training of logic, act with precision and comprehensiveness, both in the matters they handle and in what they refuse. Most minds have slid away into various approximations to insanity, or are in stages of only partial recovery therefrom.

Had thought the precision and certainty of light in its action, all minds might not come to the same conclusion in matters taken up for study, because of different antecedents or from occupying diverse points of observation. A road travelled in one direction, looks very different upon retracement. But travelling the same road, though in opposite directions, two persons can talk intelligently of its scenes and way-marks. And life does not present stand-points so wide apart that the parallax of any, and especially trans-mundane objects, amounts to much.

Yet how diverse the modes of thought and opposite the views held on almost any subject. Take any art of livelihood, any mode of business, any department of philosophy, æsthetics, or politics; why, from the same premises, do men come to such different conclusions? Why does not the "mechanism of thought" act with the precision and certainty of light? Then, when we come to the highest of all themes, religion, we find widest diversities. How much these are increased by the moral states of the thinkers, cannot be definitely told. These bring their aggravation, no doubt; but perverted mental action has its influence here, as in business, as in arts, philosophy, æsthetics, and politics. And when religion is taken in hand, the Kingdom of Evil finds an element of success in perverted mental action.

It is in confirmation of this that men do not hold religion to be the highest theme open for study and as including man's true welfare. It can be proved to be just this; yet what proportion of men hold it in such esteem? If it has the warrant of reasons, why do not all thus hold it? In this age of material improvement, how, for success in business, is consideration of religion put aside? Not merely are religion and business held in antagonism as conflicting interests, but business is put in ascendency and religion held subordinate. Justification is sought for neglecting any interest of religion, or violation of solemn vows by one plea,—"I was busy," or, "Business prevented." Success in business, in accordance with the moralities of religion or in contravention ot them, is held paramount to all claims of religion by so many, that the Kingdom of Evil finds an element of success in the perverted way of thinking now current.

This idolatry of business was not always dominant as now. Time was when men were afflicted with no such craze of worldliness. Once, men were interested in the study of philosophy. Never in times of speculation has business, or politics in presidential canvass, taken such possession of the minds of men, as questions of philosophy have. Time was when a whole city cared most "to hear some new thing." Such questions occupied the thinking of the age. Under banners of philosophy, parties were marshalled. Men congregated to hear lectures on philosophy, as now to transact business in chambers of commerce. Men went abroad to study questions of philosophy, as now to carry out some scheme of commerce or railroad enterprise. The great men of those times were not "railroad kings," millionnaires, nor merchant princes, but men of letters and philosophy.

In another age chivalry was the great thing, and gave the age its ruling bent. Humanity in all its specimens was measured and weighed by the chivalrous spirit found in each. Wealth was nothing, even learning nothing, save as that wealth was consecrated to chivalry, and that learning gave the chivalrous spirit a more gallant tone. This was not the amusement of the dissipated few who were above the hard necessity of work; but, like fashion, it took possession of society in all its ranges, just as the material progress of this age keeps all poorest men toiling and sweating for betterment of fortune.

Even religion has been the great absorbing interest of an age. Men were thought of, not as rich or poor, but as adhering to this religion or that. Not territorial enlargement of kingdom, not a favoring balance of trade, not monopoly of commerce, but establishment of this religion or that, was what arrested attention and occupied discussion in royal cabinets. What was schemed for by kings, and striven for by nobles, was discussed by the people. Never has business and material betterment in this age shown itself more dominant and all-pervading, than in some former age has religion; less, however, as a law of life, than as a scheme of doctrines, and still more as a state policy. It was the politics of the age, ruling the thoughts, making itself the burden of all chief discussions, and even the rallying cry of battle.

That was long before there came this present craze of worldliness under which we now suffer, and which some think as a perpetual infirmity under which the race has suffered in all its ages. The human mind will not always follow one bent. Varieties of fashion are attempts at escape from the dulness of a treadwheel round. Present greed for gain has not always been, will not always be, the ruling passion. Some have reached freedom from it, even now. That it is now the ruling passion, cannot be denied. To develop the resources of the world, and especially of this New World, of all waste lands and waste forces, has place in the great schemes God is carrying on. But this strain will not always last. It will give place to the better things for which it is providing. While it lasts, it is not strange, that, to minds perverted in their action and helped to no enlargement by faith, business should be held in conflict with religion, and paramount to it; and that thus the whole subject of religion should be overlooked by the many suffering under constricted mental action; nor that hereby the Kingdom of Evil finds success.

But to those who give religion any thought, vicious ways of thinking give the Kingdom of Evil further elements of success, by misconceiving the very nature of religion. One would expect, that in its essential nature, it would be found a very simple matter. It is not simply for the learned, the wise, for men who have leisure to study and speculate on high themes and abstruse subjects. It is also for men who must maintain a daily fight against starvation, who have stomachs that cannot be neglected, and skins that must be protected against weather. It is for men whose minds have never been liberalized by study, who have no gifts for nice distinctions; for men who cannot give exact definitions, and are not versed in profound thought.

What, then, would we expect religion to be, unless God meant to tantalize us with it? A very simple matter, coming within comprehension of unlettered men, capable of being grasped by men unused to subtleties of nice distinctions and abstruse speculations, and even by children. It is only a right life instead of a wrong life. All men live a life; every one is compelled to know how to do that; and religion is only a life rightly lived. As a life, it takes in all the contents of life, demanding them to be right and fitting to the relations sustained.

The senses show man in his relations to his fellows. Religion, then, must involve a rightly-lived life in all relations to them. Here come into play all the graces and moralities arising from loving his neighbor as himself. In these relations he acted before, it may be with a supreme regard to himself. But loving his neighbor as himself, he will do unto others as he would have them do to him; and so one whole table of the divine law is obediently fulfilled. What is simpler to conceive than this changed mode of life? He keeps at work the powers whose use has filled up his life so far, only he uses them in a different way, under another principle, and with a new spirit.

While the natural powers show man in his relations to his fellows, faith shows him in his relations to God. He is still to live a life; religion only requires that it be rightly lived in Godward as in other relations. And what do existing relations to God require? Simply that he accept God as revealed, the Creator and Supreme Ruler, the Redeemer and Saviour of men; trust him as the Redeemer, love him as the Saviour, and obey him as the Supreme Ruler. This involves repentance for sin, faith in the atonement for sin, a humble and prayerful Christian life. Religion in practice is simply to accept the situation, to take the facts as they are, and live accordingly. Taking our surroundings as they are, comprehending truly the soul's relations, estimating rightly its powers, and putting them to fittest use, religion becomes the most fitting and reasonable life a man can live.

Yet on no subject are the minds of men more befogged. This comes, in part, from lack of thought, and from a blindness which sin somehow begets. However intelligently the gospel has been preached to men in the years of their former history, when they come to see their sinfulness, to apprehend their danger, and seek to enter the way of salvation, the ordinary inquiry is, "What shall I do to be saved?" That a pagan jailer in Philippi, who had never heard a sermon, should make such inquiry, is not strange; but that it should be the standing inquiry of men accustomed to hearing the gospel, shows either a strange lack of thought, or a blindness of mind, which sin in its universally damaging power brings upon the purely mental activity.

Misconceptions in religion come in part from wrong instruction; but that is only to trace the difficulty back one step, where again we find the mind working abnormally, falling into perverted habits of thought as it comes to handle religion. So is it in the larger half of the nominally Christian church; where religion is not a life lived, as the word of God and the nature of the case clearly show it to be, but a work done, *opus operatum;* and once done, even supererogative, a basis for indulgences; so much religion accumulated, just as well-spent toil is so much capital created.

Clearly where such misconceptions prevail as to the

nature of religion, the Kingdom of Evil will find in such errors an element of success. The opposing interest to the Kingdom of Evil is the Kingdom of Christ. Nothing limits or restrains the one, except the other. In the Kingdom of Christ, religion is a life rightly lived by the soul, that soul's right action in all manward and Godward relations, that soul's right use of its powers, a personal quality. That perverted mental action which misconceives the nature of religion, which makes it a work done, capable of accumulation by religious acts, as capital is by industry, finds no use for itself in the Kingdom of Christ, belongs to the Kingdom of Evil, and in that Kingdom is a large element of success. For there are millions on the earth who hold this misconception, represented in that Ecumenical Council at Rome, plotting to hold the world to the ideas current in the Dark Ages. Theologically, organically, and numerically, here is a large element of success in the Kingdom of Evil; indeed, no inconsiderable part of that Kingdom, as organized in the world, is to be found in that hierarchy, under which a perverted mental action holds religion to be a work done. To this view we are reluctantly compelled by the known character of the papal church, without denying that it contains many Christian people, and without opening debate as to what that church may yet become.

Misconceptions of the nature of religion may be expected whenever the mind is perverted in its action, and that is wherever sin is working its damage. Not as a life rightly lived in all Godward and manward relations, but as a work done, religion is held by many an adherent of Protestantism. Perhaps in every Protestant congregation, and without close search, men can be found who have hope of final salvation, yet are without any intelligent view of what constitutes religion, and poor success in reducing to practice what religious convictions they hold. It is plain to others, if not to their own dull minds and duller consciences, that they have failed to enthrone the first principles of religion to authority in their minds. They keep on the level of ordinary moralities with such success as those sinners have who go in good society. As to anything characteristically religious, it is entirely wanting, beyond a few religious observances, as to go to church with the ordinary regularity of fair-weather attendants, and supporting the institutions of religion in a way whose meagreness and dilatoriness give sore trial to others' patience.

Beyond the proprieties of ordinary morality, they find one other proof of Christian character, lying away remotely in the history of former years, when conscience was stirred, fears aroused, and feelings excited in a way quite unusual. In this general disturbance on the subject of religion, they opened not their hearts to God's regenerating grace, and repentance did not turn them into the ways of Christian living. Felt unworthiness led to no trust in the Redeemer, loyalty of heart to no consecration of themselves to God and his services. They found no adjustment to a prayerful, humble, and Christian way of living, no adoption of gospel principles as a law of life, no opening of the heart to the indwelling of God's Spirit, and, in consequence, no joy and peace in believing.

At length their convictions wore off, their fears subsided, their excitement died away, and, under much mental confusion, they followed others in joining the church. Instead of making good their Christian profession, they are found living on the same principles, for the same ends, and in the same spirit as before. Essentially they are the same in character; yet they have had an experience on the subject of religion, which they counted becoming religious. They imagine religion to be a fact in their history, a thing done, though hardly amounting to any supererogation, and to this they come for comfort when the well-warranted fear arises, that life gives no characteristic proof of piety.

In our churches are to be found such men; by their profession they shield themselves from that address of the gospel which befits sinners. They rely upon an historical experience, which their dull and perversely-acting minds have never analyzed to see that it was not an experience of God's regenerating grace. So they have a religion, not lived as a life, but held historically; a thing done, like the prayers and penances of the papist, and of as little value.

By such confusion of thought and perverseness of mental action, men come to misapprehend the nature of religion. What is so simple and plain that many a child comprehends it and reduces it to practice in beautiful consistency, is totally misapprehended by many, and by some consigned to the region of the unknown. Perverted mental action, working congenially with the corrupt heart, makes room for this misconception and gives it power. Clearly, men entertaining it will be safely included in the Kingdom of Evil. Let all minds come into such perverted ways of acting, then there is no room among men for the Kingdom of Christ, and the Kingdom of Evil will reach highest success.

CHAPTER X.

MISCONCEIVED UNNATURALNESS OF RELIGION.

THE Kingdom of Evil finds an element of success in the misconceived unnaturalness of religion. It involves the question: What is the true measure of man? Some conceive man to be ruled by selfishness, controlled by personal ambition, frenzied by passion, full of abominable lusts and appetites. If this be the just measure of man, — this, and nothing more, — then nothing could be more unnatural to him than religion. It is irreconcilably and eternally at war with man as thus described. If it gains any ascendency over him, it is to the extirpation or control of every passion and lust. Not strange, therefore, that some look upon religion as a system of unnatural constraint, consented to, if at all, only from fear of worse disaster in the coming hereafter.

Many thus misestimate religion. Accepted as a law of life, it would lay a check, if not a positive prohibition, upon the chosen delights of their life. The free, easy, and congenial ways in which life runs would be broken up, habits revolutionized, affinities destroyed, and the entire drift of life set into a channel which, so far as known, looks difficult and uninviting. What conscience has already said to them has been in no pleasant tone, nor upon any welcome theme. Even the voice of reason has been full of rebuke. And the word of God, whenever consulted, has been replete with admonitions full of disturbances. Now, to commit self to reason, conscience, and the word of God as the chief advisers and authoritative directors of life, has no one element of attraction.

They are confirmed in this by the testimony of Christians. True, these Christians sometimes speak of joyful hopes, evidently based upon a superstition as to what the future contains. What they say of present joys and the conscious experience of blessedness, comes evidently from a self-wrought fanaticism. But these are not the burden of their utterances. They tell of fears, conflicts, and failures to realize their impracticable ideal. With these come self-condemnations and self-torments. The few and faint approvals of conscience are overborne by its terrible denouncements. They bewail oftener than bless themselves. By the weight of their testimony, they have chosen a comfortless lot, where fear and anguish are their nearest neighbors.

Men holding this view of life and Christian experience, confirm themselves in their convictions by that expression of the apostle, "If in this life only we have hope, we are of all men most miserable." From which they infer that if there is any good in religion, it is not to be found in this life, but in some future state, concerning which they ask, Who knows?

Even if a little out of the order of thought, it will help on the discussion to inquire how Paul came to say this. From other parts of his writings we know how he esteemed the wealth, pleasures, and honors of this world. He counted them as nothing for the joy and hope he had in Christ. He had tried the world under the most favorable circumstances admissible in his age. More than most men he was able to grasp its advantages and enjoy its benefits.

In the light which revealed Christ to him, an exposure was made of the littleness and meagreness of this world as a portion to satisfy man. By that light there was revealed to him the profound depths of the human heart. He found that the mind had a grasp, a breadth and height of reach, a capacity which nothing but the Infinite and Eternal could fill. He found within himself not only a use for all the contents of the universe, but a need for all there is in God himself. Convinced of the inadequacy of what the world has to offer as a satisfying portion of the soul; having found in the hopes and foretastes of gospel blessedness that which could excite every power of the mind to highest activity; that which could stir the emotions to their profoundest depths; that which opens to thought loftiest range and widest sweep; that which could call out the soul's utmost love and devotions; that which enabled the soul to find its true place and normal condition in the surrounding universe and under the moral government of God; its faith taking hold on God and securing all the practical benefits of infinite wisdom and infinite power; the troubled conscience finding in an atoning Saviour such perfect peace, "that the thunders of the law become an anthem of righteousness"; the divine love in Christ meeting the soul in terms of reciprocal appeal and response, and hope taking possession of all the contents of a good and grand immortality; then to have all this stricken from the heart, as death of hope in Christ involved, this would leave the apostle consciously far more miserable, pitiable, than the sinner who had never discovered the profound wants of his soul, nor the emptiness of the world as the soul's portion.

It was not because his heroism had been tried by persecution; not because he held himself to any drudgery that was not self-ennobling, nor because he had so long foregone earthly pleasures; but because in the rays which shone around him from the throne of God he had seen the depths of his own heart, taken measures of his capacities, and had come upon an intelligent conviction that this world, with all its varied contents, could not fill the depths of his heart nor occupy the capacities of his soul.

In that light, which a hope in Christ shed around him, Paul discovered longings, felt stirred within him a consciousness of power, had excited an activity of thought; more than all, felt a capacity of love to be given and received; all of which demanded the infinite and eternal, and demanded right adjustment with God through an atoning Saviour. Shut away from all this, as the loss of hope in Christ involved, no more could he come back and build a resting-place for his soul with the perishable materials of this world, "make him gods and find them clay"; no longer in hearts already stricken with death, and, worse still, corrupted by sin, could he find objects to call out his love, nor fountains of that return love, which, as a bath of refreshment, he needed to have around him forever.

There is another measure of man than that which they apply who pronounce religion an unnatural and cheerless constraint; a measure which recognizes him as endowed with reason, conscience, and immortality; a spirit capable of divine inspirations, a subject of God's moral government, having a reach of mind and depth of heart which have use for all contents of the universe and all perfections of God. Till thus seen, man is not seen aright. His reason must find a God,—a God of such perfections as are revealed in the Scriptures. Beyond all second causes he finds room for a Great First Cause, a Self-existent and Eternal Jehovah. The more man fathoms the depths of his own heart, the loftier the height and the wider the sweep of his thoughts, whether among the materialities of nature, the records of history, or the depths of philosophy; the more comprehensively he comes to understand society, government, humanity, and the possibilities of the future, so much the more pressingly does he feel the need of just such a God as rules on high, and who ought to be, if he is not; for who else can give any hopeful outcome to what is going on?

Equally, there should be a law of infinite righteousness; nothing less than the perfect character which meets that law can satisfy man's reason. He may fail, all around him and through all ranges of history he may find only failures to reach the character demanded by that law; still, with nothing less can reason be content. Even despair of success cannot justify him in abandoning the attempt. Such is his present condition, and reason affirms that so it will be eternally.

Reason may never have anticipated the Plan of Rescue revealed in the gospel; but it is found fitted to all deepest wants in man, to highest capacity and intensest longings. Only by denial of his relations and surroundings, by ignorance of his wants and capacities, can the gospel seem abnormal. It is in felt adjustment to man's conscious wants and anticipated necessities.

So far from being unnatural, artificial, and forced, the Christian life is normal, fitted to man's powers, adjusted to his capacities, and consonant with his highest longings. On the other hand, if there is a constricted, unnatural, shallow, delusive, and unmanly life to be found in the world, — a life that leaves man's grandest powers undeveloped, his deepest emotions unregulated, his strongest impulses ungoverned, his truest humanity uneducated, and his noblest energies slumbering in him, — that life must be found within the Kingdom of Evil. In all that is said and done to entice men from that Kingdom, it is not to bring them under unnatural constraint, but to emancipate them into their truest freedom; not to starve mind or heart, but to feed them with angels' food; not to sadden a life, now sorrowful enough, but to give true and eternal joy. The end, and not less the means, can be justified. This is not theory; it has historical verification. Human experience thus far has not been for nothing. Some things have been settled, and among them this, — that the gospel supply fully meets the human want.

No human mind can comprehend the varieties of the human condition. We have general terms, which mark certain obvious and salient points of that condition; rich or poor, virtuous or vicious, honorable or degraded, civilized or savage; these are general terms, without precision and definiteness. Under each is a wide diversity. We sort men in lots, and have terms of description only for the class. We fail to get the grand product of variety, unless we take each individual as a factor, making account of natural endowments, opportunities, culture, incentives, temperament, experience, and resultant character.

Yet to all this variety the gospel addresses itself, comes to each as just the help needed. No man has risen so high, sunk so low, or wandered so far out of the ordinary human condition, as to be beyond the reach of the gospel. No man has filled his heart so full with the schemes and success of ambition, with the toils and rewards of industry, with the longings and requitements of human love, with study and mastery of science, as not to have in his heart ample room for the gospel. Men have been endowed with the richest gifts of genius and talent; have had all culture of science and art; been helped by health, wealth, and favoring providences; have started from levels in society whence they could quickest reach the heights of success; yet, as they have taken measure of their capacities, heard all voices of want crying out of their hearts, and looked into the possibilities of the future, they have confessed there was room in their hearts for the gospel's work and the gospel's reward.

So, at the other extreme of the human condition. If he be a man of failure and untoward fate, when the deranged machinery of life has brought its heaviest crush upon him, not so has his heart been filled with grief and gloom, care and concern, distrust and despair, fears and forebodings, that no room could be found for the gospel. Take the most pitable wretch, found in lowest depths because fallen from high position. Beginning to fall, let foe and former friend help him downward. Let treachery betray him, poverty starve him, and false friends turn him adrift homeless. Let every calamity stick fast to him, every misfortune hedge him about, and every disaster bring its crush upon him, till this modern Job shall curse the day of his birth. More yet, by far, take away from him the heroism of integrity, the inspiration of uprightness; weaken him with the consciousness of moral degradation; crush him with a sense of guilt; let every horrid fear beleaguer him, remorse sting him, and coming retribution appall him.

Such men there have been. Can the gospel do anything for them? Into such hearts the gospel has come, removing the sense of guilt by the assurance of pardon, dissipating the fear of retribution, the love of Christ filling the heart as no human love ever did. Though such a man could not recover the good repute he has lost, the friends he has alienated, the possessions he has squandered, and the health he has sacrificed, — yet, in the depth of his poverty, in outcast loneliness, amid tortures of disease, yea, in prison and chains wherewith violations of civil law have bound him, he has sung a sweeter song, been filled with truer and richer joy, than has the world's favorite.

Between these extremes, among all classes, from the man of highest success to the man of remediless failure, all who have come to any just apprehension of their powers and capacities and wants, have found need and room in their hearts for the work and reward of the gospel, as much as any of highest success or worst failure; for the need of religion grows not out of the accidental conditions, but out of the essential nature of humanity.

The Creator of man is the Author of the gospel; and he has instituted between them an adaptation both comprehensive and minute. In man there is no longing, hope, weakness, or fear, which the gospel does not meet; no power, of which it does not make the most. In the gospel there is nothing wanting, nothing superfluous; for it there is no substitute. It deals with man, not simply as an individual, but puts him into society; permits all affinities of worldly interest and social endearments to cluster around him; and in these gives such wisdom to his intelligence, such restraint to his passions, such incentive to his powers, and such tone to his spirit, as to make possible to him the highest good.

History gives warrant for what is here affirmed. Through the ages and to-day, the gospel is doing just the work humanity needs. None are beyond its reach; none exempt from its claims; none independent of its help. In illustration: From humblest condition of life, by rapid yet legitimate steps, aided by the genius of American civilization, a man went upward, till he stood at the head of this nation. By the helm he stood in the stormiest passage of our history. Never were hands so full, mind so occupied, or heart so burdened with weighty cares. 'T would seem that his occupation was use enough for one soul. Every interest of the nation, in urgent and tumultuous throng, like centring waves on ocean rock, beat about that Presidential Mansion. Swift couriers came and went; messages forth and back on wings of light ning. The decision of battle, the issue of campaigns, the fate of millions, the solidarity of the Union, and even the life of the nation were involved.

Was not that use enough for one man? Could not such occupation push aside God's claims on his personal love and obedience for four years? Could not such absorbing interests and weighty cares so fill every capacity of thought and feeling, as to make that heart forget its need of forgiveness through the blood of Christ, its use for a hope of heaven? No, no. There was room in that occupied heart for the gospel, need for all its work, want for all its reward. Away from the perplexities of state, away from the anxieties of war, the hand of a sick and dying boy led that father into another world of thought and feeling, — not a new world to that habitual attendant at the sanctuary, that diligent student of the word of God, that man of deep and earnest thought. There he gave and took what bound his heart to Christ in the exalted hope of a Christian man.

To-day, in meanest abodes, where poverty yields

its full fruitage of wretchedness, where starvation makes cheeks pale and lips thin, where the chill of night keeps nigh at hand the coldness of death; in homes where worldly cheer has not smiled for many a month, where disease has weakened the arm that brought them bread; in homes through whose window death and famine look in familiarly, disputing which shall enter first, — in such homes may be found Christian patience, a joy and cheer that hushes all repinings; may be heard voices of prayer that utter many a sentence of praise; may be found hearts that throb quick in responsive love to Him whose death opened the way to the many mansions he now makes ready; may be seen eyes made brilliant in hope of the glory to be revealed, — in such homes may be found a dying mother, leaving little ones, whose cry of sorrow hunger has made weak, giving them to her trusted husband, and all to her trusted Father in heaven, longing to stay and comfort her husband and train her children for heaven, yet longing to depart, counting life's bitter experience a joy, since it has brought her to a death-bed where angels wait, and made her home of wretchedness an entrance-room to the heavenly mansions.

The light of day that exorcises the "dream of darkness," the protection that gives peace by day and safety by night, the cool water that quenches the thirst of fevered lips, the loaf that staves off starvation, the store laid up that hushes all fear of want, the culture that lets into all God's world of truth and beauty, human love given so lavishly and its sweet requitement, — room and want for these, not more than for rectified standing under God's moral government, hope of forgiveness through Christ, peace of conscience, the way of believing, and an intelligent hope of heaven.

There is nothing superfluous in God's universe. Every soul can use its contents, needs its range, to live in its eternal light of truth and beauty. There is capacity in every soul for all Christian graces, an answering thrill for every fear, hope and joy that centres in the Infinite and Eternal, room for all contents of the gospel, need of its comfort in the years of life and in the hour of dying, need of its guidance through life and amid the possibilities of the future, need that it hush the distractions and quell the disturbances of sin by reconciliation with God through Christ, need of the personal sympathy and love of Jesus. In no soul has this need been more pressing than it can be in any, than it must be, if life end not in failure. If there is anything fitting, natural, and normal to the soul, it is the religion of Jesus Christ.

Yet to many — O, how many! — a Christian life seems a forced state, unnatural to all the genuine play of the soul's powers, a constraint upon its readiest action, its deepest emotions, and highest aspirations. Still, if, upon advisement of Him who has control of affairs in this universe, religion is seen to be necessary to eternal welfare, it can be maintained, borne, endured, met like hard-earned and ill-spared payments on an insurance policy, — yet it is to them an artificial and forced constraint. When proposition for entrance upon a religious life comes squarely before them, they look forward to it as painfully unnatural, to whose duties they could adjust their lives only with manifest awkwardness, under whose influence life would have a frigid mechanical aspect, not merely dull and dreary in negations, but positively irksome with its constraints. This unconceived unnaturalness of religion, so largely prevalent, is, beyond debate or need of showing, a fruitful element of success in the Kingdom of Evil.

CHAPTER XI.

DENIAL OF ETERNAL RETRIBUTION.

THERE is a sense of justice in the human mind. It may be said to be constitutional, innate. This has been denied. As well deny that speech is innate because the child cannot talk. That may properly be said to be innate or constitutional, whose rudimentary germs are found in us, sure to come to maturity and power with normal growth. Early and always justice shows itself, when the mind comes to mature action, and even before. Let wrong be done to a child, and in the resent awakened an impulsive and crude sense of justice is expressed. As the mind approaches maturity, the sense of vindictive resent abates, turbidness subsides, and the sense of justice gets cleared of all base and foreign ingredients.

That in this sense of justice there is not necessarily any feeling of resent, is evident from the fact, that its voice is equally imperative when wrong is done to others. We see advantage taken of the weak and helpless by the strong, of the innocent by the artful, and we instinctively demand justice between the parties; vindication and, if possible, restitution for the wronged, punishment for the aggressor, even though we have no personal interest in the transaction. We demand justice, not from fear that if wrongs go unredressed there will come to be a corrupt state of society, or that oppressors will become bold and overbearing, and we suffer in consequence; but we demand justice to satisfy our present and innate sense of what is right.

This sense of justice enters into the structure of society, just as the law of gravity enters into our way of handling material things. If a building, constructed without reference to the law of gravity, would come to ruin, not less would society without the law of justice. Yet it is something more than a wise prudence in guarding against damage in the social and civil relations of life. Without reference to advantage or pleasure, every rightly acting mind demands that justice be done. Even the heathen could say, "*Fiat justitia, ruat cœlum.*" Even against self comes this pronouncement of justice. Having done wrong, it may be to our advantage in manifold ways for justice not to interfere; it may promote our immediate pleasure for justice not to hurl retribution upon us; yet we feel we deserve it. And till justice has adjusted the wrong, we feel that the matter is not finished. Men have even sought courts of justice and charged themselves with capital crimes, rather than bear about the guilt of unavenged wrong.

If, however, the fitting penalty is fearful in degree, as the death penalty for murder, men whose humanitarianism is in the ascendant and whose sense of justice is dull, may recoil from inflicting it. Others, of tenderer sympathy and duller sense of justice, may refuse to sentence the murderer to imprisonment for life. Men, in other respects whole, are incomplete in their sense of justice, as others are in their sense of the merciful or the beautiful. Such incomplete, abnormal men abound in society; indeed, the difficulty is to find one not marred by some defect. If a man disposed to do justice finds himself to recoil from inflicting the penalty, he may go back to reconsider the crime, to take measure of its magnitude, not to inflame his vengeful feeling, but that his sence of justice may come to healthful tone. This done, the penalty affirmed, as befitting the crime, can be inflicted with a steady hand. If there be failure here, it is because compassion has weakened the sense of justice.

Justice is a necessary element in all forms of society. Take society in its simplest conceivable form, two men living on an otherwise uninhabited island; justice would need to be there with her adjustment of mutual and individual rights. She demands room in the family, the church, in voluntary associations, in incorporated communities, in the state and nation. The larger the social combination, the more intricate its relations and the greater the magnitude of its interests; so much more the need that justice have the handling of its affairs.

In the moral government of God it is readily seen that justice and righteousness must be the foundation of his throne. What organization so vast, what relations so intricate, what interests of such magnitude! Considering either the perfections of God, or the necessities of his government, we expect here to find justice perfect in degree and unfailing in its certainties. While history gives us only hints of this fact, revelation sets it before us with distinct emphasis. If shown that it finds not simply here and there an illustration, but that it runs through every intricacy of relation, it wakes no surprise. Indeed, such pervasion of justice meets the demands of reason. We even dare to say that God's moral government has no right to be, unless founded on justice. Infinite and eternal wrong has no right to rule. No emphasis of denial can abate our conviction, that justice, infinite and eternal, must and does have room and sway in the moral government of God.

In that government, who but its Divine Ruler can manage its administration? What eye, save the omniscient one, can see the consequences of conduct, or trace where wrong will end? None but God can fix the penalty befitting wrong. He alone can measure its guilt, comprehend its principles and spirit, its exhibitions and effects. Into the spirit of the sinner God looks, finding what would overturn his throne of righteousness, but for the restraint of impotence. In the consequences of sin God sees ruined souls, yea, a ruined universe, but for the restraints under which he holds sin. Whether it approve itself to our short-sighted wisdom or not, God has fixed the penalty of sin. If it approve itself to our wisdom, well for us; but if not, it should awaken no surprise; for we have not come up to his point of vision, nor gained his sweep of thought. He has done it without our help and will execute it without our hinderance. Here we find the stabilities of justice.

In the administration of his government, progress must be made, results must be reached; to finite minds contingencies must give place to certainties. So God has made the doings of this life to issue in character. How long the series in which such doings and results are only single steps of advance, no finite mind can tell. To something greater, the progress we see may be only what the revolution of the earth on its axis is to its sweep around the sun. But be it only a step in an infinite series, or the final product of all history, character is formed by the doings of this life. So much we can see, even if only the segment of a circle which we cannot trace.

With consent or without, every man must put himself into drill. Some fashion or fixture he gives to moral character by every act. And act he must. In this rush of life he cannot stand in immovable stolidity. The constant appeals made to him he cannot meet with an indifferent non-committalism. Wants will draw, necessities impel, whatever point they involve.

And this is what we see men busiest at. Alone or in company, in sickness or health, at home or abroad, in success or failure, the one thing men are busiest at, what they never cease from, during all the hours of conscions existence, is drill in character. By action and non-action, in consent and refusal, in what they receive and reject, by use and misuse, they are giving form or confirmation, tone and touch, to moral character. It may be without plan or purpose, it may be against fixed determination; still they must ceaselessly work at this stint. What is prosecuted so untiringly will at length bring some definite result. It may be an occasion of joy or sorrow. It will be something positive. Character comes in such incomprehensible variety, that we may not always be able to detect its definitive traits, — may not have discernment to sort each with its kind; but the all-seeing eye of God will make no mistake in the final assortment. Indeed, each may affiliate with his own as by instinct. Only with his own sort will the righteous have any fellowship. Only with the reprobate will the finally impenitent seek companionship. Fearful as such a doom may be, still less will they be attracted to the holy. Even in this life they give distinct intimation of preference for anything than fellowship with the godliest.

To the righteous and sinful character God has affixed consequences that are eternal. The biblical teaching on this we give only in summary. To each he has assigned a condition whose duration is expressed in the same terms. Hell is as permanently built as heaven. A condition of wretchedness must expect to continue as long as the sinful state out of which it grows. Men are seen to be sinners till death takes them in hand. The presumption is, as divine revelation teaches, that moral character continues in the next life, as formed here, with the addition of confirmation and progress. All arguments, showing that God will in some future stage of history rid the universe of sin because of its oppugnance to his character, are as pertinent to show that he would never have permitted its introduction. For this we know not his reasons, and so cannot affirm that those reasons will abate. The reasons for its permitted introduction may be equally reasons for its permitted continuance.

If men will sin, they consent to its preadvised results. These may be very inadequately apprehended. They are as much beyond the reach of human comprehension as is sin, their cause. Just such infinite quantities are in man's handling, and he hesitates not at the responsibility. He lays his hand on the shaping of character and the fashioning of eternal destiny as carelessly as though it were the amusement of an hour; and ceaselessly is he busy at it.

When, however, we come to any proximate view of the consequences of sin, as seen in its wonted results in this life, or as seen by faith in the divine declarations as to what is coming hereafter, the mind is appalled with their magnitude and terribleness, and even seeks to rid itself of the fearful impression by denial. Let one go through the wards of a penitentiary, note carefully the conditions of those incarcerated there, trace them back to former life, see the station in society they occupied, their domestic affiliations, notice what powers of mind are held in restraint, withering in disuse, perhaps becoming palsied with idiocy or frenzied with insanity, and he may instinctively say, this is too terrible. Counselled simply by sympathy for the imprisoned, if he might, he would quickly unbar their prison doors.

But let him look at the matter on the other side, trace out the history of their crimes, burglary, arson, robbery, counterfeiting, seduction, murder, not in the generality which their names present, but in the particulars and aggravations of wrong, injustice, and cruelty which each presents; let him notice that those crimes were not the unwitting impulse of some heedless moment, not the distraction of some quick and sore temptation, but the last fatal plunge in some long career of unrighteousness and even of lawlessness; let him note the fairness of their trial and the righteousness of the law under which they were condemned; then will he see how all the joys of life, the securities of home, the value of reputation, the pleasures of fraternity, the conditions of progress, the possibilities of high attainment, and the solidarity of society, would be swept away if such laws were not enforced, and such crimes were rampant. Taking counsel of justice, the completeness of benevolence, and not taking counsel merely of sympathy; rather, giving the sympathies their true range, and caring wisely for all human interests, and for all law-abiding citizens, who outside of prisons are pursuing their lawful occupations without infringement of others' rights; and he will find abundant reasons why those prison doors should remain securely fastened. Hard as the lot of its inmates may be, instead of diminishing, he would add to the securities of their prison, and, if need be, re-enact the laws that condemned them.

All this is on our level and within reach of our comprehension. These crimes against the security of property, against the peace of society, the value of reputation, and the sanctity of life, we can understand. We see how far they would go, what damage they would work. We know what is necessary for their restraint, and feel not only justified, but even impelled by all highest considerations, to put such crimes under penalties proportioned to the magnitude of the interests against which they make war. This is justice, and we cannot consent that it should abdicate its rule.

When now we lift this whole matter up to the level of God's moral government, we are compelled to confess that it passes beyond the reach of our comprehension. How far sin may go, where evil will end, we cannot tell. The welfare of the universe is as far beyond the reach of our comprehension as its magnitude is beyond the power of our measurement. We can conceive that all highest interests of the universe may rest upon the security of God's throne; that in the real and seen righteousness of his character is there any stability to the universe or any safety to its inhabitants. We see, therefore, that his character and government must be in eternal and infinite opposition to sin in all its forms, degrees, and manifestations. The interests he has in charge require this. He is a God of infinite responsibilities. Whatever may be necessary for the protection of these interests, to keep lawlessness from ascendency, and misrule from anarchical devastation, this must be, whatever else is, or is not.

It is not submitted to our approval what penalties shall sanction God's law, what eternal consequences he has attached to sin, or what doom he has assigned to the finally incorrigible sinner. From what little we know of sin, as it shows itself in this life, we are justified in the conviction that its consequences hereafter will be bitter, wretched, terrible, past all comprehension of our thoughts. As we might expect, so God's word affirms them to be, summoning all forms of known suffering to depict their misery, making it yet more terrible by the added announcement that it will be eternal.

There is no truth of God's word, however plain, positive, and repeated, which has not met denial. Distempered by sin, the mind can meet with denial any demonstrated truth of religion or any instinctive conviction of moral consciousness. This is the plague of sin; so, when the eternal consequences of sin meet denial, that truth only fares as other truths of God's word have. Unable to comprehend the enormity of guilt, to measure the magnitude of sin, to conceive the vast and varied interests of God's moral government, such denial of the eternal consequences of sin is only what might be expected. And it is made, sometimes by peremptory denial of penalties, sometimes by affirming that the penalty is found in the disrepute and disasters immediately consequent.

There is still another view to be taken. God is greater than anything he has done, more than anything he has made. Even the universe does not measure him, nor its interests balance his. Sin is against God, wars upon Him, instigates rebellion against his government, plots his overthrow, and but for the restraint of impotence would realize its ends. To take in the measure of sin, then, the mind must comprehend what would be done by the realized intent of sin, by its reaching the success at which it aims; what God's dethronement and universal anarchy mean. This is beyond the grasp of human thought; equally so is sin.

If, then, God assigns a penalty to sin that staggers the faith of unbelieving minds, it should be no wonder. They have no conception of the magnitudes concerned. Not always revolted state of heart, oftentimes constricted range of thought, lead to denial of the eternal consequences of sin. If men deny the plain revealments of God's word, and the deep longings of their souls, by consenting to annihilation, to rid themselves of the conviction that the penalties of sin are eternal, it harmonizes with the blindness and perversity which sin induces. Yet such denial is made, sometimes held and advocated as an article of belief. Even a religion is made of it, and a religious sect is organized upon that denial as a characteristic and central article of belief. That denomination has churches, a ministry, and literature. They make themselves known and heard chiefly in denial of the eternal penalties of sin. This they do without comprehending the drift of sin, without being able to take measure of its magnitude,—as no finite mind can, —without understanding its intent or estimating its enormity. This they do in denial of the perfect justice of benevolence and often by minifying sin, as though what has flooded the world with woe, and cost God the death of his Son, would be a trifle.

This denial has not always such daring. Often it exists only as a vague and unexamined feeling, refusing to be confronted by reason, to put itself into the handling of argument, or to accept with docility the teachings of God's word. And yet it has positiveness to mould the convictions and give tone to feeling. Hereby a man is placed in a very different attitude towards God, his word, his government, and the future. He takes not a meaning from the word of God, but imposes one upon it. So let there be a firmly settled conviction, or a vague, yet perversive feeling, that matters will come out right in the end; that when the incitements to sin found in this life shall pass, selfishness and sin will somehow die out; that God's justice will abdicate its authority and "let by-gones be by-gones"; thereby God, his government, and the future, are made something very different to such a man.

He is in a false relation to the realities by which he is surrounded. He endangers his soul; not more could he endanger his body by denying the fact of gravitation. Realities become unreal to his mind, idle fictions are the basis of his calculations, and he builds the hope of eternal welfare on a foundation of sand.

Here we come upon another element of success in the Kingdom of Evil, — this denial of the eternal consequences of sin, a denial, either in announced and defended convictions, or in vague and unexamined feelings, of the eternal penalty which God attaches to sin. Let this denial exist in the mind, either as a tenet of belief, or as a mere sentiment of the feelings, and how safely is such a man included in the Kingdom of Evil. Other and higher reasons there are why men should abandon the Kingdom of Evil and enter the Kingdom of Christ; but so low is the level to which most have fallen, that these are neither apprehended nor appreciated. The life of sin, which comes so handy, gives no token of coming retribution, and so makes no alarm. In sin he sees no danger. His moral energies are in no array against it, further than the proprieties of life require. He calls himself to no conflict for victory over it. To it he sees no penalty affixed, save perhaps the disrepute, damage, and discomforts found in this life, which he has already learned to brave and bear. So he utters no cry to God for mercy, softens his heart in no repentance, feels no need of a redeeming Saviour, opens his heart to no regenerating and sanctifying spirit. Safely is he in the Kingdom of Evil.

Put to devising a Kingdom of Evil and ruin, opposed to Christ's Kingdom of Righteousness and salvation, charged with introducing into it such elements as would give it respectable success, this one element would be essential, if not sufficient. Fear is as legitimate a motive as hope, but let a denial of the consequences of sin become universal, and what alarm could stir the fears, or what promise excite hope?

Not only could such a denial be an element of success in the Kingdom of Evil, but such it is in reality. It is not merely a possibility, but a fact; and the success which it gives to the Kingdom of Evil is equally a fact. Of this terrible fact, illustration can be found in every community, and in all times hitherto.

CHAPTER XII.

DENIAL OF DIVINE FORGIVENESS.

A FLAW in a diamond, or a fleck in an emerald, abates its value, though such defect might not be noticed in coarser stones. The soul is such a high and beautiful creation as to be beyond appreciation of the coarse judgments formed under sin. What mars it is counted a trifle, as fitly the mote that inflames the eye and destroys the sight. Some never found in the soul a capacity for all knowledge, a need of faith reaching beyond outmost bounds of knowledge; never found in the soul an appreciation of all most beautiful and sublimest things that can be; never found in the soul a use for immortality, for all contents of the universe and all perfections of God. Such find no capacity in the soul for reciprocal thought and affection with minds of loftiest range, still less of concurrence in thought and emotion with the Infinite Jehovah.

Naturally, therefore, they minify sin, and see not that it forbids the soul so grand a destiny. When the gospel represents the soul as in a lost condition, they withhold assent. They deny the need of God's interference with a scheme of salvation; they pass by the earnest endeavors and strenuous conflicts necessary to recovery out of the snare of sin. Or if shut up to something of this, as the way of reaching betterment and success in this life, they deny the need of any radical revolution of moral character, or of any so intangible a thing as divine help; and so utter no cry for it in prayer. They seek betterment — salvation, they would hardly call it — under law, but not by grace.

No such general drift, no such quickened interest have thoughtful minds found, as now, in studying "the reign of law." Some view of the sphere and authority of law, even most superficial students of nature find. This is among the first lessons of infancy. Fuller instruction comes with all subsequent experience. If any success is reached, man is compelled to heed the laws which so irrevocably determine his conditions and surroundings. To some study and recognition of law he is forced by necessities which he cannot escape. He learns, because compelled under threat of disaster and failure.

But more tractable students are found. Profit offers its incentives. There is wealth in these secret laws of nature. Mining here pays as well as in auriferous mountains. The hidden forces of nature can be utilized for betterment of the human condition, both to meet grossest and most imperative wants, also to beautify and adorn. And wants reach as high as this. Not alone in provision store and clothing shop are human wants met, but as really in stores of art, knowledge, and beauty. So entrance is gained into secret cabinets of nature. Wide range is here offered and accepted. Retort and crucible are put to use. Inquiry and experiment exhaust their patience, only to rest and try again. Earth's secret stores are pryed into, her witnesses put to closest cross-questioning, so as to gain some more facile way, quicker result, larger and surer reward.

But nature has, if fewer, yet more devout students. They search not for profit, but for truth. To them what is true is greatest and richest. Not for enlargement and certainty of profit, not for betterment and beautifying of outward condition, not to meet the demand of pride, nor even the cry for help. They wait and watch all secret entrances they can find into nature's mysteries. They try all her locks and bars, and could they find nature off her guard, they would not hesitate at burglary. If nature draws a veil over her distant works, they will wait, patiently sitting out the night; or go on long pilgrimages to better posts of observation. If nature is slow in some of her processes, they will wait upon her moods, and give her all the time she asks. If she is particular about quantities and temperatures, these shall be graduated to infinitesimal measurement. But all her tricks of combination and resolution, the way she spins and weaves her threads of light, their composition, as they stream from sun and more distant star; how she tones her voices, utters and echoes her sounds; how she turns motion to heat and back again; what equivalents she has established; what the multiples of her combinations; indeed, whatever is true must be known. Nothing so far, so great, so hidden, so microscopic, but it must submit to the handling of analysis. Hindered by no awe, or more reverent for knowing more, these men of science push their researches into nature's arcana, and if they can, into whatever mystery she has, back to protoplasm, and would gladly subject life itself to analysis.

So far as they go, throughout the entire range of their discovery, they find the reign of law. The further they go into nature's temple, they find, not deeper gloom, but more delicate shades of light and cross-light, laws more intricate and subtle, yet universal, differences of result traceable to differences of combination, or seeming exceptions, the working of a higher law. Law reigns with absolute supremacy through all the wide range of God's works which the senses can explore. Even when the senses call to their aid instruments of research, which most ingenious and nicest art can furnish, so as to take up smallest atoms, or subject to criticism objects hidden away in stellar regions, the senses find the worlds of materiality under law.

What expectation does this create, when we come to that higher realm of God's works where thought, conscience, and moral affections have their action? Here also we look for law, and here we find it enthroned in power. As, in the material worlds we found not the principles of hydrostatics governing the motion of light, nor the laws of chemical combination ruling the reverberations of sound; but everything under the sway of laws adapted to its nature: so in God's higher realm of mind and soul we expect to find laws fitted for government in moral action.

Thought has its laws not less than sound; conscience not less than light; moral affections not less than chemical combinations. Gravity holds the worlds together with a pressure not more constant than that which moral obligation brings upon souls.

Only under law can life have any meaning, the soul an intelligent history; only under law can conduct have significance, or character take shape; only under law can aims be prosecuted, purposes be realized, or ends reached. In the moral department of God's works, law is not less necessary, nor less imperative in its authority, if things that are find any worthy use or even justification.

In the realm of materiality, the reign of law, holding the order of nature to its wonted course, realizes only an endless series of reproductions, mere treadwheel motion. The forces of nature keep their own level, can rise no higher. Outside of this ceaseless round the laws of the material world contemplate no advance and effect no progress. They act as well as they ever have, do as well as they ever can. They offer us the same help as they did to nations of remotest antiquity, and will offer no more to most distant generations of the future. In this no consummation is reached, no purpose served, except continuance and multiplication, which gives existence no justification. The mind demands something more, if its capacities are ever met. Only in the unrest of progress can the mind find rest.

History responds to this demand, and affirms a progress. In the arts, in government, in civilization, and in all institutions of society, which are facts as stubborn as nature can produce, progress is seen. History testifies to this advancement on every page of her record; and did not this progress show itself reaching into the future with more comprehensive plans, the highest incentives to action would be wanting.

Upon historical warrant, from the nature of mind, and to meet the demands of humanity, we look for laws in the moral department of God's works, adapted to the natures they are to handle. These are beings unsatisfied without progress and endowed with the power of non-consent, a power found in no range below man. With this non-consent put into execution, the conditions of life are changed. Laws there still are, even more than before; now, not only a law of righteousness and life, but also a law of sin and death; and given a place, accepted, not less surely will the law of sin and death work out its results, than would the law of righteousness and life had it remained in sole authority. Enthroned in power, consented to, there is a fearful certainty in the law of sin and death.

The laws of the material world can be observed, thus keeping ourselves within the lines of safety and welfare, or they can be braved, and we rush into various perils. So of the laws ordained for the government of our moral nature. The possibility of violating them has become a terrible fact. Every intelligent, self-conscious being of our race has violated the laws of God's moral government. The only exception the world has known bespeaks itself Divine.

All laws, ruling among the materialities of nature, are found invariable in their action. They insist upon bringing in their consequences. These may be trifling or terrible, yet they are not to be overlooked, — none so trifling as to be neglected; none so terrible as on that account to fail of infliction. On the higher level of moral action, does not law insist with equal pertinacity upon all its consequences? If a wounded arm give pain, will not a wounded conscience? Deranged secretions bring disease; will not perverted affections mar the health of the soul? If its sure working and inevitable consequences indicate the value of the law and the worth of the interests it defends, we may look for certainty in the action of moral as of natural law.

Diseased action in the body brings suffering, and that suffering is chronic if its cause be chronic. The painful, labored gasping for breath does not restore the congested lungs to normal action. Pain does not mend the fractured bone. So, while passion rules, while the mind grovels in animalism, and selfishness perverts the affections, the sufferings that come in consequence will not neutralize and correct the perverted action of the moral powers. So long sin, so long suffering.

To what, then, are we shut up? Under the law of sin and death we clearly are by nature. Is there possible to us only such a destiny as sin will bring? Must violated law rule our future with its terrible certainties? To this some consent, reconciling themselves to it by minifying the consequences of sin. What cannot be endured they hope will be abated by the Divine Mercifulness. They hold it to be even a matter of honesty with God, that he should bring on every sinner the exact consequences of violating the law. This is only another illustration, to their minds, of the imperative reign of law; and it is to them a matter beyond dispute, that whatever consequences law assigns must come. Their deliverance from the consequences of sin is simply an endurance of them. Into the iron hand of such a hard necessity they give themselves. They are made content with this prospect, only because they see no other results of sin than the immediate damage and disrepute it works. Sin has its immediate inconveniences. Angry emotions disturb the peace of mind. Resents entertained embitter the feelings and give a disagreeable fit of moroseness. All such violations of moral law, even if confined to the heart, inflict pain and do a worse damage by blunting the sensibilities. Wrong once done, remorse must be felt, till conscience is deadened; and this, not because we are fools, but because we are men. And these evil consequences come with the certainty on which law always insists.

Then, if utterance be given to hate, and curses be profanely invoked, the disrepute of it brings a recoil of shame, and bitter self-chiding does he get for having made a fool of himself; and these he bears as the penalty of his wrong. His abated self-respect, and the consciousness of his disrepute in the esteem of others, are stings that remind him of his violations of law. If his hate has gone forth in the infliction of wrong, then retaliation smites back, or the wrong is avenged in the courts, and smarting under the retaliative blow, mulct by the court, or sent to prison, he meets a penalty which he counts the exact measure of his guilt. If pride has swelled to ridiculous proportions, or his ambition has overleaped itself, so that he is made a laughing-stock, in this chagrin he suffers, perhaps keenly, and counts that the penalty. If covetousness has got the mastery of him, enticing him to expose property to dangerous risk for the chance of larger or quicker gains, and what he calls luck be against him, the loss he meets he may take as the penalty of his covetousness,— more likely, only as a rebuke of his folly in incurring risks.

When a man has made himself a slave of avarice, breaking down his health by hard work, and has at fifty years of age undermined a constitution that should have kept him hale twenty years longer; when unregulated appetite and injudicious feeding, accompanied either with sloth on the one hand, or overtaxed energy on the other, have brought upon him the dyspeptic torments of a guilty stomach; or, when riotous living and intemperance have thrown him into an earthly hell of *delirium tremens*,—in all such cases the sufferers find the sure operation of law, and probably count their sufferings the adequate penalty of their sin. Counting these physical, personal, social, and temporary consequences of sin its fit penalty, finding in sin no guilt but what can thus be measured, and regarding these, by the imperative reign of law, unavoidable, their philosophy shuts them up to a consenting endurance of consequences, which they regard adequate penalties. Thus the matter is rectified. By suffering they count themselves to have atoned for their guilt. The affair is adjusted, and they stand on the ground of recovered righteousness. They feel no need of a gospel, no need of an atoning Saviour; see no room for pardon. Indeed, they hold that even-handed justice, perpendicular honesty, forbids pardon, and insists upon the penalty, which the unobstructed reign of law brings.

Some have thought this out as their theology, others hold it vaguely. Yet it has taken deep hold of their feelings. They are governed by it, are shut away from the gospel by it, giving no earnest heed to what is revealed to them as a way of salvation. That great central fact in history, the Incarnation of Christ and the Redemption he wrought out, is nothing to them. They find no room for it in their hearts. They make no confession of sin, offer no plea for pardon, utter no cry for help, and gird themselves to no struggle for deliverance from the power of sin. There is an element of success in the Kingdom of Evil.

There are immediate and unavoidable consequences of sin. They are not its penalty, do not measure its guilt. When such consequences have been endured, whether they pass with the hour that chronicled the sin, or ran on through all future years of life, — these results, passing, leave not the soul in moral standing and quality such as before. The man thoroughly cured of *delirium tremens*, in his bodily state, in his tastes, appetites, habits, associates, estimates, in any way by which his quality can be tested and measured, is a very different sort from the man who never made any approach to that terrible abyss. The endured consequences, penalty as he counts it, and what he calls his recovered righteousness, place him not back at his first starting-point; that he can never reach again till history shall undo her record.

Sin is not only subjective but objective. If wrong be done, the aggressor arrested, condemned in court, and sent to prison, he may bear the rude penalty which civil law attaches to his crime; but therein he bears not the penalty of his sin, nor makes adjustment of matters back into the order which his sin disrupted. The house he burned, the men he crippled, the virtue he sacrificed, the prosperity he ruined, the life he took, are not restored, even if he abides in the prison till the grave be ready for him. Man can do wrongs which he can never right. The adjustment he can make and his recovered righteousness,—the one is as unreal as the other.

The temporal consequences of sin are not its penalty, because of disproportion. Judged by its temporal consequences, a sin often costs less than a blunder. A mistake, where the parties supposed they exercised due care, brings two railroad trains into collision; property is wrecked, men crippled for life, others hurried out of the world, leaving wives widows and children fatherless. How costly a blunder can be! Wearied with long watching at the bedside, the mind, under some paralysis of fear, or stupor of drowsiness, tries to rally its attention to the care and responsibility of giving medicine. He thinks he has roused himself to needful care, but memory or attention fails, he gives the wrong medicine, which makes sure the advent of death. It was only a mistake; but how much more than some sins, in immediate disaster, a blunder costs. If measured by temporal consequences, how much more are some mistakes than some sins; how much more they mar the peace, order, and welfare of life; how much more fearful the anguish, more terrible the suffering they bring upon a community, than do some sins. And yet blunders, mistakes, do not ruin souls, even if they destroy life. Only sin ruins souls.

If such be sin, if moral law reigns as imperatively as the laws governing matter, and if consequences come as surely in the range of moral government as on the level of material forces; if the penalty of sin is in proportion to its enormity, as both reason and revelation affirm; if the guilt of sin is to find measure in the penalty, and so transcends all that can be contained in this life; if the penalty, even when its duration occupies eternity, works no adjustment of the wrong the soul has done, and so brings not the soul back to any recovered righteousness, then how terrible the condition of any sinful soul.

Is recovery possible? Or whatever possession the Kingdom of Evil gains, must it be held irrevocably? Recovered innocence is impossible to the sinful soul. A right act does not neutralize a wrong one, and restore the soul to its former state. The murderer, who afterwards saves a life from impending destruction, does not cease to be a murderer in fact or law. Once entering the way of sin, then, under the reign of law, is not the way of return effectually barred? So nature affirms, and law. Through all ages, over all continents and islands, we look in vain for any movement of humanity realizing a recovered righteousness. Under no incentives of nature, by none of its impulses, will the natural heart move in that direction, even when pushed by the bitterest consequences of sin. And while the soul is in the mire of guilt, by the reign of law it is hedged about with consequences which make the unsought way of return more impassable.

But there is a Power higher than nature, higher than man, higher than law. He who made nature and man and law, while he cannot annul the verities of history, can modify the resultant effects, can arrest the fashioning power of the past, and give the soul a different future. In doing this, as a governmental procedure, he finds justification in a divinely wrought atonement. He can break the dominant power of sin in the soul. The everlasting reasons for righteousness, the infinite urgencies which an interminable future presents, and the sway of a divine impulse, can reconstruct a soul and regenerate it into a new life.

Law still reigns, but the conditions of its action are changed. Incentives to evil are abated; incentives to righteousness are augmented. As in winter, so when summer comes, law reigns. Where were the coldness and rigor of death, are the warmth, the beauty, and vigor of life. Law has not abated its imperativeness; yet under changed conditions, law, in its absolute reign, gives summer, with its life, beauty, and fruitage where before were only the sterility and death of winter.

The gospel can bring the soul into God's summer. When the beams of the Sun of Righteousness shine into the heart, there is a relenting, as in the thaw of spring; tears of repentance begin to flow, obedience germinates, hope blossoms, trust in the Saviour gives the blossom of life, and the inspiration of the Almighty fructifies the soul. This changed condition brings around the soul, even under the reign of law, incentives to which, before, it had been dead, and leads it to purposes to which, before, it had been averse. New conditions of life exist. There are new relations Godward, manward, and all around; and things before impossible, now come freely, naturally, and normally in the historical life of the renewed soul.

If, now, it be a fundamental law, that God treats things according to their nature, then that renewed soul will receive very different handling, because of its very different nature. If forgiveness, fully arresting the penalty of sin, be bestowed, and the assurance of it begotten in the soul; if now that soul draw near to God in prayer, in fellowship, and the sweet reciprocity of love, instead of being shy of God as before; if now self-seeking, before so dominant as to make the soul ugly in its selfishness, give place to a careful regard and just appreciation of the rights and welfare of others; if now range be given to thoughts, feelings, longings, and purposes, reaching out to the embrace of the infinite and the eternal; if the realities of faith are the range of the soul's life, and love the controlling principle, — and under the gospel all these may be, — then that highest law of God's Kingdom, illustrated in every field of human knowledge, that he treat everything according to its nature, comes in and secures for the soul an entirely different destiny.

Here is the work of God's gospel. By it souls are brought out from the law of sin and death, into the law of spirit and life. These laws reign as before; but the regenerated man has passed from the deadly power of the law of sin, and come under the quickening power of the law of life. In his changed character God can treat him differently, not in violation of the supremacy of law, but in accordance with the law that all things be treated according to their character. This is the divinely-originated and divinely-inaugurated scheme of salvation, including in it forces that regenerate and sanctify the soul, and a pardon that arrests the penalty of sin. Such a gospel is the great and blessed fact testified to by thousands in every age of Christian history. This is the vital principle in that Kingdom of Christ, which has been set up in this world, the only antagonist to the Kingdom of Evil.

But this, men will not accept. Blinded as to the nature of sin and the reach of its penalty, attaching to sin no penalty save the immediate and inconvenient consequences that follow close upon the heels of transgression, they accept such disasters as the full penalty of sin, and count that penalty sure of infliction under the imperative reign of law. They find no room for the gospel, see not the higher laws of God's Kingdom, and have no comprehension of the reach of his love. So they are safely included in the Kingdom of Evil, and that Kingdom finds an element of success in denying that the Son of Man hath power on earth to forgive sin.

CHAPTER XIII.

DOMINANCE OF SOCIAL INSTITUTIONS.

IT stands to reason that all interests are to have place and consideration, are to secure endeavor and co-operation, according to their importance. All the interests of the Kingdom of Evil are such as foretoken for it failure and ruin. Yet just contrary to what all rightly-acting minds would have supposed, instead of coming to the failure and extinguishment it deserves, it has come to a pervasive power, so far readily called success. This fact needs to be borne in mind throughout this discussion.

The Kingdom of Christ, opposed to the Kingdom of Evil, has use for all human powers and agencies. So rich has the Divine Ingenuity made life to be, that all the individual powers and legitimate organizations of social life have place and use in the Kingdom of Christ. Its claims harmonize with all things that have a right to be, can make these subservient to its ends and put them to their highest use. It sanctifies to its aims every human relation, gives exercise to every power, and direction to every desire. It has a place for the individual, use for all that he can do or become; a place for the family in all its ways of fashioning character, and a place for all social relations in the sway they have over conduct and destiny. Here is room for personal influence and example, for the exercise of personal gifts and graces, and for all the industries of Christian endeavor. Here is room for the family and state as divinely ordained, and for all the voluntary associations which Christian ingenuity can devise and justify.

Among the institutions which the Kingdom of Christ has devised and perpetuated, and by which, so far as human efforts help, it gains advancement, are public worship and the preaching of the gospel on the Sabbath. Herein men have their attention directly called to the salvation of the soul from the dominion of sin. Herein are presented views of life, of the soul's relations, of the grand contents of the future, very different from those usually held before the mind in ordinary life. Herein are presented considerations very different from those which usually sway men. Herein the mind is led to an outlook upon all greatest things within its survey. What is true and right, infinite and eternal, that with which the mind has mainly to do, the substantial business of life, transcending all else with which the mind can meddle, — is here presented in ways most favorable for candid and persuasive consideration.

Among organized institutions the church stands pre-eminent, as the chief agency for establishing and extending the Kingdom of Christ; and of all her methods of action, Sabbatic worship and the preaching of the gospel are the chief. The organization of the church, and the institution of the ministry, were for that end. In theory such was the design, and in history such has been the practical working of the forces divinely organized in the Christian church. Where these forces have had unrestrained action, they have proved their wisdom.

Whatever, then, hinders attendance upon the preaching of the word and the worship of God in the sanctuary on the Sabbath, is an element of success in the Kingdom of Evil. It may be dull preaching, poor singing, an uninviting sanctuary, the lack of prompt, habitual, and interested attendance of church members; but whatever secures only desultory attendance, and leaves large classes in every community in non-attendance, proves itself an element of success in the Kingdom of Evil.

And here comes up a remarkable fact, worthy of serious study, — the difference in attendance upon divine worship among the Protestant and Papal churches of this country. As a rule, all Papists attend church, ordinarily with regularity. If it must be in poor clothing, at unseasonable hours, or on days given of God for labor; these are to be no hinderance. If long distances have to be travelled, in modes of conveyance that are wearisome, if prompt payment of church dues be demanded, these are to be no hinderance.

How is it, now, among Protestants? Many never go to church at all. Men who have looked into statistics on this subject, affirm that a large part, if not a majority of Protestants, do not attend church as a habit; that only a small percentum attend habitually.

Indeed, the Protestant church edifices now standing would hold only a small part of the Protestants in the land. These churches may be near, within half an hour's walk or an hour's ride, to reach them, costing only the relaxation which every healthy man needs; the seats may be free to all who will occupy them; members of the church may stand at the door and give hearty welcome to all; yet the attendance, however large in the aggregate, is meagre in comparison with the whole Protestant population. As in some churches, there may be no dues to pay. While all Papists, even poorest servant-girls, pay their dues, there are probably in every Protestant congregation to be occasionally found men who dress well, live well, and in ordinary affairs mean to pay their way, but who attend church in their irregular way, year after year, without paying a dollar to meet the varied expenses of the sanctuary. Others would be welcome, if they would only come. And then in many communities there are no sanctuaries, wide reaches of country, well settled, yet with no house of God inviting attendance.

Why this difference in Protestant and Papal attendance upon worship? No one or two reasons are sufficient. Certain causes govern in some communities; others, elsewhere. Prominent among them these may be found: —

1. In this matter Papists have pushed a truth into an extreme that has made it an erroneous superstition. Made to act through the senses, it is true that our senses can aid us in worship. The visible and felt presence of others in a sanctuary hallowed

by sacred associations, bowing with us in the same confessions and supplications, uniting with us audibly in the same songs of praise, knowing them to be thrilled, humbled, and exalted by the same truths that stir our hearts, — all these give a power and impressiveness to the preaching impossible elsewhere. There is an impression of the truth, a sense of divine things, an appreciation of the gospel, which can be got only in a sanctuary filled with devout worshippers. No secret worship, no private meditation, can stir the soul, quicken its emotional graces, and lift the heart heavenward, as is possible in a large assembly of worshippers.

This is not a peculiarity of our religious nature. It is so on all levels of life. The highest enthusiasm in any common interest, and the loftiest patriotism, are called forth when large bodies of men are moved by a common appeal. There is power in the exercises in which large numbers participate. This is not the entire warrant, but it enters into the reasons for public worship and the preaching of the word in the sanctuary.

Here is enough to justify the use of places consecrated to public worship. Papists have pushed the use of sanctuaries to the extreme of a superstition, by affirming that certain religious acts, as under the Old Testament Dispensation, though singly performed by an individual, have a power, validity, and worth because done, or when done, in the church; at least that their power, validity, and worth are greatly increased when performed in a consecrated sanctuary. So they flock to the church to do these things, and to get other things done for them by the priest.

2. Here comes another reason why Papists are held to church attendance as Protestants are not. To them their minister is a priest. He can do for them what they cannot do for themselves. These, to be most efficacious, must be done in church. And as, in their view, these are necessary, if not to salvation, at least to Christian burial, by considerations which their minds keenly appreciate, as also through the power of the confessional, they are held to church attendance as Protestants are not.

3. Then, again, Papists are not offended by any contrasts presented by wealth and poverty. They accept the condition in which they were born. If they are poor, if they are servants, they accept the situation. As they are, they are willing to appear. They make no idle pretence to what they are not. No poorest or shabbiest of them take offence at the presence of the rich in gay clothing, even if they take not a little consequence to themselves for belonging to such a congregation. Poverty bars them not from church. They are not troubled with the ambition that inflames the Protestant world. They have not that upward reach of the Protestant mind that makes each ambitious of all that any has, or has done. With Protestants, each must be the peer of any. The exalted condition aspired after is not in moral character, not in personal culture, but in visible condition, generally advertised in dress. So if at church they cannot make show of equality with the average, their Protestant pride will protest

against church attendance. This is humiliating, because true.

In whatever the Papal devotee may fail, it will not be in attendance at church. Even Italian brigand or Spanish freebooter, familiar with robbery and even murder, is careful not to be remiss in going to church or observing saints' days. So of the poor; if they must clothe themselves from scantiest wardrobe, they permit not pride to take offence, and suffer not themselves to be detained from church by any arguments pride may urge. Let one take his stand at the doors of any Papal church or splendid cathedral; while he sees wealth enter with costly robes and gay adornments, poverty follows without hesitation. Here "the rich and the poor meet together; the Lord is the Maker of them all." It would seem — and may we not hope — that they go to present themselves before the Lord, fully advised that the Lord looketh on the heart and not on outward appearance. Whatever may be said to his discredit, past all dispute it must be admitted that the Papist is a faithful church attendant, each in such garb as befits his means. If he might worship more intelligently, scarcely could his worship be paid more habitually, even if more devoutly.

Looking into the churches of Protestantism, or rather about them, we find a marked contrast, not simply in the fact that so many stay away from church, but also in the forces that bar them from attendance. The facts and the way they come are plain enough.

Churches are built so costly in structure and adornment, that the poor can have no assignable portion, often no place, in them. To get the funds necessary to erect a church elegant enough to meet their taste, the church members must secure the aid of wealthy sinners, who also have a taste to be gratified in its design and details; and for their investment they want a specific return in a pew, to be held as private property, subject to the general use designated. This makes the cost of pews too great for ownership by the poor. Even if some ineligible pews are set aside for their free use, they are not accepted, because it would be an acknowledgment of poverty, of commercial inferiority, which, even if true, they care not to acknowledge at church or on the Sabbath.

But why not as well there and then, as on the street and during the days of the week? Just because in such conditions they do not acknowledge it. Capital is not master more than labor. Indeed, labor rules capital as often as reversely; lays down laws for capital as often as capital for labor. In all places of business, and through all the days of the week, labor stands as firm in its dignity, as independent in its freedom, as capital can. And if there comes a contest, victories are not all on one side.

A few free seats in a church whose eligible pews are held by the rich, or even a free gallery, must fail, not only because inadequate, offering seats for only one in a hundred; but more surely must fail, because on the Sabbath, the laborer's day of freedom, and into the Divine Presence, it brings the distinct notification of commercial inferiority, and that means, also, social inferiority, if not vassalage, — a notification which capital would not dare to whisper on week-days and in places of business, where labor can maintain its dignity in conscious equality. In aristocratic countries, where there are four or five distinct layers of society, pew ownership may do for those who can afford it, and a few free seats for the poor may succeed; but not in this land of freedom and equality.

Trammelled by this vicious system, yet uneasy because of its virtual exclusion of the poor from God's sanctuary, some seek to rectify the matter by building mission chapels for the poor, retaining the costly sanctuary, with its ornate embellishments, as fitting their more elegant tastes, their more refined society, and their more exquisite worship. Many will go on a journey, but not to heaven, in second-class cars. Cheap places in which the poor may worship, without disturbing the rich in their elegant and costly churches, will never, in this country, correct the Protestant habit of neglecting the sanctuary.

The true principles of church building — churches large enough to afford seats to all the families within reach and not otherwise provided for; such seats free from personal ownership, taxed only for necessary expenses; or, better still, for half that amount, the balance to be raised by voluntary contribution — have not had extensive illustration in this country, but must, or this Protestant habit of neglecting the sanctuary will never be broken up.

There is growing out, as an excrescence of our culture in this age, a certain exquisiteness of religious life. Ritualism is one extreme of it. But it is confined to no denomination. It is a failing of human nature at a certain stage of development. It requires that all the appointments of the sanctuary should have the nicety and finical adornment of a parlor; that the exercises of worship be conducted with courtly precision; that every movement of the minister be with Chesterfieldian propriety; that sermon and prayer be in purest Addisonian rhetoric; that the music be operatic, even if an unintelligible jargon to many, and that it be rendered by a few distressingly-cultivated voices.

Religion becomes a matter of *eclat*, or is nothing. Unusual ceremonial in the church secures large and prompt attendance. Men are eager to hear titled dignitaries, and are early on hand to witness any imposing array that shall captivate the senses. The æsthetic element is made to predominate over the moral. The church is a Sunday theatre; its exercises an entertainment; decorum the chief grace; the sentimental will do; the sensational takes best; most pertinent truth, stupidest of all.

When matters of taste, no longer the mere adornment and fitting drapery of a high and earnest life, become central and are the chief thing of thought and aim, they occupy a place which deranges the order of life, giving chief importance to what is only incidental. Under the reign of this spirit, costly adornments of the sanctuary and a style of dress among church attendants prevail, putting to shame all who have more pride than grace, and barring them from the house of God. If in the census of the United States last taken, the question had been put: How many times, during the past year, have you stayed at home from church because you "had nothing fit to wear"?—true answers would give surprise.

It is an easy matter to prove that these are not justifying reasons for staying away from church. But this is not a matter that gives itself into the handling of argument. It is not a matter of reason, but of feeling. If reason should lead, the feelings would not follow. Prove to such men, that they thereby affirm the body to be less than raiment, and the soul less than either; they may disown this degrading estimate of their manhood and of the soul's dignity; still, pride will not go to church except on terms of equality. The cost of our churches, the style of dress in our Christian congregations, and the reacting pride of those who will not attend church in conditions uncomfortable to their equanimity, are elements of success in the Kingdom of Evil, working for its increase and strength at the very point where the Kingdom of Christ puts forth its most aggressive action,—the public worship of God and the preaching of his word.

Here is a dominance of social over religious institutions. When the usages of social life require one thing, and religious obligation another, the former prevail. This involves what the mind is very prompt to deny, if stated in the abstract,—that man is more than God, social laws paramount to divine ordinances. Let the obligation of social hospitality solicit one to stay home from church or the prayer-meeting, and the sacramentally sworn vow is broken, under requirements of social courtesy. This shows a hollowness and nervelessness of religious life, a lack of power, which puts sinners beyond the reach of the church. The sinews of its strength are cut. Spiritual life is environed and encrusted with a counteracting social life.

Nor is this confined to personal service and the use of time. It is seen in the use of money. The usages of social life demand money for adornment and style of living beyond the requirement of fitness. These can, with many, be met only by rigid restraint of expenditure in church enterprises and benevolent contributions. Charities are withheld that pride may be gratified. Social institutions dominate over the religious, thereby strengthening the Kingdom of Evil.

The contest for ascendency between the Kingdom of Christ and the Kingdom of Evil is not fought out in the great reforms and revolutions in which nations engage; it is not carried on simply by the great movements which absorb the attention and enlist the endeavors of Christian denominations; nor by the advances which education and civilization make, even though the Christian life act and utter itself in all these. The contest covers all lengths and breadths of life, reaches to its widest compass, and enters into its smallest particulars. By all ways in which thought, feeling, and purpose express themselves, in all ways by which sway is exerted by mind over mind, by everything giving tone to feeling, reach to thought, guide to conduct, and shape to character, this contest is carried on. Largely has the Kingdom of Evil made social institutions an element of its success, even at points where their legitimate use would be wholly in the interests of Christ's Kingdom.

CHAPTER XIV.

INADEQUATE PHILOSOPHY OF EVIL.

IN this world all great interests have advocacy. At first thought, only what is good, right, fit, beautiful, and beneficent would be expected to be upheld by argument and commended to observance by earnest pleading. The simplicity that expects only what is befitting will meet with many a surprise. What is immediately profitable, let it be as wrong as possible, will have advocacy. Slavery has rejoiced in many an able and well-constructed argument, earnestly pleaded and masterly handled. Polygamy has earnest advocates, not only among men, but — strangest of all — among women. If none have been found to urge intemperance as a duty which every man owed to himself, yet all the customs, arts, and appliances which lead to it, and to nothing else, have been defended as respectable. Even houses of prostitution have been defended as necessary evils.

If vices so gross and harmful have found advocacy, much more would we expect the Kingdom of Evil, which includes with these other things less exposed to reprobation, might have, if not formal advocacy and set arguments of defence, at least apologies, drawn in the name of forms of good, assumed by it oftentimes.

Evil as well as Good, Wrong as well as Right, has its philosophy. The Kingdom of Evil, as well as the Kingdom of Christ, has data for a philosophy. It has facts, causes, antecedents, consequences, incentives, appeals, rewards, all the data necessary for a complete and practical philosophy of Evil. It has powers of moving men in all the ways of their activity. It can exercise the reason, arouse the imagination, excite the fancy, appeal to the judgment, tax prudence, bring all passions into play, and give the conscience enough to do. It can stir hopes, awaken fears, and indeed give some scope to all natural powers in man.

A system so comprehensive and distributive has vast ranges for thought, can find exercise for any talent, and open wide fields for all varieties of genius. To put things to their wrong uses will try ingenuity not less than to put them to their right uses. To systematize the Kingdom of Evil will test the powers of talent and genius not less than to systematize the Kingdom of Good. Fully to educe all the powers of Evil so as to make the most of them, will require as much thought, experiments as varied, as much empiricism, and as earnest persistency, as to educe the powers of Good. Here, in this Kingdom of Evil, there is room for bulkiest literature. It is in proof of the world's modesty, or its downright dishonesty, or else of an instinctive reverence for the Good, that all the world's thinking, and the literature it has begot, really in the interest of the Kingdom of Evil, is not so labelled.

The many in the Kingdom of Evil stay not in it upon warrant furnished by any Philosophy of Evil, formally drawn out and clearly stated. And yet it seems to them that they have reasons for their course. They have graduated into life on so low a level, that they have no conception of the wealth of knowledge afforded them even by material things. Some acquaintance with the laws and properties of matter they are compelled to have, as a condition of physical livelihood. Even more than this they seek by an instinctive hunger for knowledge. But even men who have devoted their best powers and a long life in the search, have not explored all the mysteries of nature, even in one department, still less the sciences thus illustrated. Coming up from the level of material things, how vast the range of knowledge which covers the action of mind in all its powers, relations, and affections! Here is room for study, which none have fully explored. In such narrow range as most men occupy, no comprehensive Philosophy of Evil has been constructed, justifying the Kingdom of Evil and warranting adhesion to it. For such adhesion men have thought out few justifications. Of mind, as capable of exploring all facts of nature and of comprehending all laws of science, art, society, and government, they have no true estimate. They see not the range and reach of its powers. Correspondingly meagre must be their Philosophy of Evil, and its principles of conduct without justification.

But there is more than this. Beyond what can be known with scientific exactness, beyond all bounds of knowledge, the mind can go on wings of faith. Belief is as normal and necessary to the mind as is knowledge. What is believed is as true, and may be as blessed, to the mind, as what is known. The soul that only knows, and never believes, has as meagre a life, is as far from full and healthy development, as unfitted to give its powers exercise, as disqualified for filling its relations, as would be a soul that only believes and never knows. Superstition is no falser a guide than skepticism. It is as legitimate for the mind by faith to take hold of the Infinite and Eternal, of Divine Existence and Authority, and of the verities of spiritual and immortal life, as by the senses to take hold of material things. A Philosophy of Evil that has no reference to the infinite and eternal verities of God and Religion, fails to justify the life it would authorize.

There is another direction in which to look. Things are getting done, and history is chronicling her record, which she permits no sacrilegious hand to expunge or even modify. Something is going on. Things have been, are, and will be done. There is a drift and direction in the movement of humanity. The past is not for nothing; the future is to be something more than a repetition of the present. God has a hand in affairs, pushing them on. As was to be expected, he has, in history, made disclosure of what man needed to know; has done what is necessary, that man might make the most of himself and reach the highest exaltation. This includes recovery from the fall into sin, the re-enthronement of reason, peace of conscience, the joy of believing, hope of immortality, allegiance to the revealed principles of the Divine Government, adjustment to right place in the universe, and recovery into the Divine Fellowship. The Philosophy of Evil, that has no such range for man, that passes by the facts of history, making no account of the past, and that accepts not the only future which can issue from such a past, is ill fitted to handle the present, in attempting either to determine its aims or to direct its methods.

With all its studies in that direction, the world has failed to develop and systematize any adequate or even comprehensive Philosophy of Evil. And considering how much it must include, the failure is not surprising. Only a few principles of conduct has it laid down, and these are neither fundamental nor of universal acceptance. Indeed, a statement of its principles in language, to a mind intelligent in the Philosophy of Good, as found in the Kingdom of Christ, would carry their own refutation. Without stopping to show how inadequately the Philosophy of Evil covers the ground to be held by a true Philosophy of Life, consideration will be given only to two of its principles, taking those of most general acceptance.

1. That material and sensuous good is to be sought rather than spiritual good; the welfare of the body rather than the welfare of the soul; the pleasures of this life rather than the joys of immortality. Such are the aims set forth by the Kingdom of Evil.

This is fundamental in its Philosophy. Not merely to the Christian, but to any sanely acting mind, its statement secures its rejection. It involves disproportions abhorrent to any such mind. Yet this principle is accepted and sways the vast majority of men. Honestly and fairly stated, these are the ends they pursue. They do not accept this as a statement of their aims, but they cannot deny them to be the very aims they seek. And from such seeking they cannot be dissuaded. The Kingdom of Evil is a Kingdom of Darkness, and here its darkness is densest, hiding from men any just and comprehensive view of the aims they seek.

This admits of thorough scrutiny. If the aims pursued by sinners have not been fairly stated, the fact can be shown. On any level of society, in any kind of business, let inquiry be made of all sinners, and reduced to simplest statement, they will be compelled to subscribe to it in the form already given; and to affirm, that, whatever ought to be, practically, in the aim of their lives, they seek material and sensuous good, the welfare of the body rather than the welfare of the soul, the pleasures of this life rather than the joys of immortality. Candor and intelligence will compel this admission.

It is only occasionally that such admission is made. One of England's boldest men of science, with the characteristic honesty of a philosophic mind, adopted and defended as true a German epigram, which made the human aim to be, "To get food, to beget children, and to feed them as best one can." The highest good which an English king wished for his subjects, was, that "every one had a chicken in the pot." All such make the aim of man to be much like the brutes, whose highest good is to be well fed and sleek; just as though "man could be groomed into blessedness."

2. Another principle in the Philosophy of Evil is, to get, rather than to give. Man took a hint or this from his mother's breast. He found within him a most imperious stomach, and that hunger kept its appointments with pertinacious strictness. In a world where life is a forced state, hardly safe when in constant defence, wants pressing upon him every hour, and passions oftener and even harder, he must have power. This he sets down as a first aim. This he finds in wealth, social position, and political standing. These, therefore, are to be sought, one or all. By these helps he would have his welfare in his own control. He would provide for every extremity that could extort from him a prayer o God or a cry to man.

And just this is what men are busy at. Stop all that is done for this end, and what abatement would the world's greed, if not its industries, suffer; how hushed would be its voices. Industries demanded by the stern appointments of want, by claims of love, and the urgencies of progress, are something; but when the lust for power has withdrawn its forces, there will be strange vacancies and silences in many places of business.

And yet how vain is this endeavor. How sweeter the peace, calmer the trust, and safer the dependence which faith in God can give! For when man reaches all the power that wealth, social position, and political preferment can give, any hour and at any place, he can be brought into straits that will extort from him most urgent prayers. So mighty are the forces that have the handling of man, that his safety can never be in his own self-controlled power.

Such men never can understand the men who live a life of faith, whose trust in God gives them peace, be the possibilities of the future what they may ; can never appreciate the men whose aim is, not to get, but to give ; to enlighten ignorance, to soften grief, to lift humanity to higher levels, to insert peace and good-will into human society, to lead the soul to Christ and ally it to God. Christianity can point to thousands of men in every age and country and in all grades of society, who have done the best they can for these ends, who with their gifts and opportunities have shown the same spirit that ruled the apostles.

They give up prospects of distinction and power, sacrifice ease and wealth, endure hardships and privations, make their lives a total failure according to the wisdom of this world ; yet with an overmastering love they bless this world, as much of it, and as richly, as they can.

If, now, the Philosophy of the Kingdom of Evil is so false, as seen in the two of its principles considered, how comes that Kingdom to such success ? The minds of men being in falsehood, what is false has power with them, as though it were true. Living in the sensible they come to believe only in what the senses can detect. The overmastering of the senses holds them in imprisonment. In the finite they find no reflection of the Infinite. And the mind that has never found the Infinite and Eternal, the man who in his weakness, wants, capacities, and aspirations has found no need of the Infinite and Eternal, who can stand and look above him and before him, and utter no cry to the Infinite and Eternal; such a man finds in the temporal and finite all the greatness and grandeur he can appreciate, rests in the finite and temporal, is satisfied with what the temporal and finite bring, is stirred by no fears, and excited by no hopes, that reach beyond the finite and temporal.

Shut in such narrow bounds, shut away from the Infinite God, finding not in the near-by immortality the eternal issues of this life, any illusion or delusion can sway the minds of such men. No most trifling fact, no lowest aim, no meanest motive, no basest desire, no sheerest caprice, no falsest principle in the Kingdom of Evil is there, that has not had sway with such men. Sunk to so low a level, where all grandest aims, all highest truths, all noblest incentives fail to reach them, human powers will not on that account cease to act. If their relations to the Infinite God and to the eternal issues of life call not out their highest efforts and noblest endeavors, yet will they act, perhaps as industriously, certainly more impetuously, under the incentives which the Kingdom of Evil presents.

In such conditions — and such are the conditions in which life, with most, ordinarily passes — men are prepared to yield to the advocacy which the Kingdom of Evil fails not to secure. The urgent reasons which pride, ease, independence, and power present for the accumulation of wealth, and the display of it in personal adornment, style of living, and spendthrift indulgences; the reasons which ambition urges for gaining place and power by any means that will accomplish the end; the reasons which perverted customs and depraved habits offer for indulging in debauchery, intemperance, and the whole round of passional gratifications; the reasons which dishonesty and laziness give for not earning an honest livelihood; or, rather, for trusting to the risks of gambling, the tricks of deceit, and to the dangers of counterfeiting, burglary, and forgery; the reasons which lust offers for gratification at cost of virtue and family endearments; the reasons which false honor and revenge give for duelling and murder; in fine, all reasons which pride and avarice, ambition and passion, vice and crime, so garrulously and vehemently urge for all indulgences in sin, have power and prevalence with men on so low a level that they have to do only with the finite and temporal as presented through the senses. So it must be till they rise up to a controlling apprehension of the Infinite and Eternal. They are where all these incentives of sin reach them and ply them with their fearful urgencies. Their faith refuses to accept the higher realities of life, by which their course might be shaped so differently. This is the most terrible fact in their condition. All these reasons enter into the Philosophy of Evil; and, inadequate as they may be, are laws of conduct to those who are in the Kingdom of Evil.

The success of that Kingdom is no matter of surprise to those who see what is put within man's reach by the Philosophy of Evil, while man is on the low level of a purely worldly life. Being on that level, men are held in the Kingdom of Evil by its Philosophy of Evil, whose inadequacy just fits their incompleteness.

With humanity in its present condition, living so largely in the level of the senses, accepting only such views of life as the natural powers apprehend, faith persistently refusing to accept the relations which the soul sustains to the Infinite and Eternal, matters could not well be different from what they now are; and the Kingdom of Evil might be expected to have its present and very respectable success.

CHAPTER XV.

PRACTICAL DISBELIEF IN GOD.

TAKING a sinful life, noting in what narrow range of thought it is confined, what a blind fanaticism, yea, insanity, sin is, we begin to see, not that there is any reasonableness in sin, but that there are reasons why souls thus blinded, bewildered, and diseased, should act according to their perverted nature. There is this sort of legitimacy in the success of the Kingdom of Evil.

In looking for further causes of this success, we can readily imagine, that if there should be in man's heart a disbelief in the personal character and positive sovereignty of God, it would be an element of success in this Kingdom. In the very idea of the opposing Kingdom of Righteousness, God is the central power and supreme head. It is for him and by him. He is its life and strength. In idea, the Kingdom of Righteousness could be nothing; in history i is nothing, save as God is in it. In the Kingdom of Righteousness, God is not some pantheistic abstraction, not the personation of some cosmical law, but a personal Being, positive a Sovereign, self-moved, autocratic, having every attribute of personality, the Fountain of all authority, the Administrator of all law,— this or nothing.

Now if from the Kingdom of Righteousness God be excluded, the Fountain, Head, Soul, Life, and Power of that Kingdom gone, there is nothing left; and ample room is made for the Kingdom of Evil. Relations exist, wants are felt, forces impel, progress is demanded, ends must be reached; and if there be no God with his Kingdom of Righteousness reciprocal to these facts and adapted to the found condition of humanity, then there is a void in the universe which the Kingdom of Evil may occupy, but cannot fill; and that Kingdom will be restrained in its success only through the limitations imposed by its own self-destructiveness.

If from any mind God is shut away as the personal Sovereign of the universe, such a godless man may respect other men of higher genius, richer culture, and broader experience; but conscious of his own self-government, and feeling in his pride capable of becoming, in certain conditions, what any are, he makes himself his own ruler, self-ruled in all things, so far as the interests of society permit. Escaped from the rule of God, he easily rids himself of all other spiritual and demoniac forces, as mere figments of superstition. In such conditions all forces of evil have their play upon him without restraint, and all ways of evil are open to him without resistance. If disbelief shuts him away from the recognized and felt sovereignty of a personal God, his culture, tastes, and pursuits may keep him on one level or another; but in all grades of his standing his autocracy holds him firmly in the Kingdom of Evil, — not by definition, but in essential fact, and beyond dispute. So far as he is concerned that Kingdom is a success, and the multiplication of such augments its success.

There are two different processes by which men come to a disbelief in the positive rule of a personal God; the intellectual and passional. These often shade into each other; since men, oftener than they are aware, are moved in their thinking by deep, yet undetected, currents of sin. Correspondingly there are two classes of unbelievers in the personality of God, — the few, who have thought out some reasons, and established themselves upon some grounds for this disbelief; and the many, who, counselled by their own lusts, find such disbelief necessary to their comfort.

1. Failing to detect in man, in society, and in the system of things existing in this world, their necessary incompleteness, men have taken offence at the crudeness, disproportions, discomforts, and antagonisms that abound. They with ready confidence pronounce these impossible in a system inaugurated and governed by a God of infinite wisdom, goodness, and power. The details of their argument, with its specification of instances, need no recital, even if there were room for them. Perverted minds repeat them from age to age, as if they had never met with sufficient answer; and thereby they confirm themselves in disbelief in the positive rule of a personal God.

If a law of progress runs through the history of each individual and through society, then on this side of highest possible attainment some incompleteness must necessarily be found. From what level this progress shall start, how fast and far it shall go, are questions no finite mind can settle. Progress we instinctively demand, not merely to escape present discomforts, but as a law of our being, in lack of which life would be clogged with the dullest insipidity. Without progress, all life, short of infinite perfection, would be cursed with an insupportable dullness. In no conceived condition could any remain satisfied three years.

There is yet more to account for what incompleteness is to be found in this world. It fitly represents to us our sin. Described to us only by definition, set forth only in verbal description, or even seen by reason and felt by conscience, no adequate view of sin could we get. It is a disturbing force, a terrible reality, perverting every heart, deranging every mind, and marring every soul. It cannot be kept from making show of itself, from exciting antagonisms, from creating disturbances and working ruin. By all these methods it reveals its nature, as we need it should, and accounts for whatever gives offence in the moral and other states of the world. Only sin is the matter.

Under the disturbance of sin no mind comes to normal action. Corrupted by lusts, made furious by passions, the mind seethes in the turbulence of its own bad state. Refusing the guidance of truth, any aberration is possible. Only that disturbance and perversion of moral action which now abounds could be expected. The vagaries of error, the fanaticism of superstition, and the credulities of modern "spiritism," are in place.

Then society, like the mind, lies close to, and takes shape from, this perverted moral action, that is going on everywhere. So arise conflicts of interest, misapprehensions, frictions, possibly a war of each with all. Sin accounts for all this derangement of society. Nothing else can. If, now, outside of the immediate province of sin, a mirroring condition of things be instituted, which shall faithfully or in any degree reflect sin back to us, so that its ugliness, bitterness, ferocity, and essential ruin be seen in the materials of nature, in the events of history, and in the condition of society, it is only what we might expect under the rule of a fair-dealing God. It meets a want in our condition, to be gratefully accepted, despite all its sufferings. If sin, then all worst things must have a place in society and history.

By this fact of sin, and the incompleteness with which progress has to do,— and if these be not facts there are no facts, — all that gives offence to the sceptic, the disproportions, incompletensss, antagonisms, and disasters find a legitimate place in a system in which sin has so much to do. Room for God is still left in this system, and what ampler room beyond, no finite mind can tell, much less deny. No fact yet found denies the positive rule of a personal God. Given sin and progress, his rule accounts for all that is; nothing else can.

Yet here are men brave in making denial of God's personal rule in the affairs of the universe, — a bravery they show which can withstand all strongest arguments of reason, all demands of highest thought, and all most earnest cries of deepest feeling, — a bravery which will never yield, save to the manifested and conquering life of Christ in humanity. So come denials of God in nature, in history, and in the revelations of his word. So come deism, pantheism, and atheism; or, in place of God are put nature, reason, cosmical law, and protoplasmic forces; any finite thing that can bewilder and puzzle us in place of the Infinite Jehovah that rules on high, so impossible is it to find any satisfying substitute for God.

Men who put themselves under the rule of such no-gods, generally feel competent of handling themselves and ruling their own destiny. What lies beyond their own control they accept as an unavoidable risk. Explore as deep as they will into nature, till they find God, they have to do only with the outside of things; till they find God, they know not what is the highest reach of thought, which is faith, nor the deepest feeling of the heart, which is religious devotion. Yet such denials are made by some minds of high culture. Some, disgusted with shams found among adherents of religion, or horrified with evils found in the world, and not having sufficient breadth of view to find place for these in the system containing them, deny that God has anything to do with this system; and not being able to see very clearly what else he has to do, they deny his personality and rule. Others, of more introspective turn, put the Divine Existence into the region of the unknown and unknowable, affirming that "the reality existing behind all appearances is and ever must be unknown." While yet others, curious in the study of the material world, have found wonders, which, though only nearer stepping-stones to God, have so occupied their thoughts that their undevout hearts reach not to Him who is above all things. So on different levels, and even in circles of high culture, there are denials of the personality and rule of God, which bring the Kingdom of Evil no small success.

2. Only a few have thought out a denial of the personality and sovereignty of Jehovah; the many who are "without God in the world," whose lives are not controlled by faith in the authority of a personal God, come into their condition by another process and in very different ways.

With some it is by constriction of thought. They see things around them in the material world, but look not beyond their most outward show. The innumerable curious things adapted to excite their wonder and start their thoughts on lines of inquiry that reach Godward, pass before their minds without arresting attention. The stones and earth upon which they tread, by their curious forms and structure, ask them to inquire what God was doing during the long geologic ages. If the query arises, they dismiss it as an idle speculation having no reference to the practical concerns of life. In all the wondrous things of vegetable and animal life, they look for no revelation of Divine Wisdom. At every step, and in every object, some token is given of God's wisdom, power, and goodness; but these stir no curiosity and awaken no inquiry. At night they look up to the stars, wondering what the morrow's weather will be, perhaps with a dull and confused sense of their distance, or with no thought at all; seldom with thought of Him whose creative fiat called them forth, and whose power keeps them wheeling so exactly in their orbits.

The earth is densely populated with such thoughtless men. They have to do only with the near-by outside of nature. Having outlived the curiosity of their early life, they accept what their untutored senses discover, as the world in which they live, and raise no inquiry as to what is above or beyond. They put things to the uses demanded by this life; skilled in the routine of business, they may even be successful in it, so as to be known as men of wealth, and, therefore, of influence; may gain position in society, and even be counted by some as its ornaments. And yet, in ignorance of the world around them, in the constriction of their thoughts, in the narrowness of their views, and in their blindness to the revelations of God on every hand, they are about as low down in the scale of humanity as any can get and maintain ordinary respectability. The grandest things about them they have no eyes to see; and the greatest thing to which they are coming is the emphatic pronouncement of their own folly.

Others come to a practical denial of God's personal authority, by the dulness and torpidity of their moral feelings. Whatever their natural temperament may be, morally they are lymphatic. So dull are they, that only sorest remorse can arouse them; so pachydermatous, that only heaviest stroke of affliction can awaken the conviction of needing something money cannot buy. Some are stolid, bestial, satisfied with being well fed. In the clamor of worldliness, all voices and outcries of their souls are drowned. To the wants of the body they gave their first thoughts, and they have cared for nothing since. Such dull men walk the earth in crowds, lifted up by no great thoughts, quickened by no high truths, thrilled by no deep emotions, and inspired by no earnest longings. Sometimes it flashes upon their minds that they are in sin; but they are used to that. With no clear view of their capacities, not knowing what is possible to them in endurance and enjoyment, nor to what achievement they can reach, troubled by no keen sense of sin's guilt and consequences, their mollusk life seems comfortable enough to them; they drone away its days asking for nothing better. Or if anything more is derived, it is only some betterment of earthly condition, to be served by further increase of wealth.

On all lower levels of life, shoals of such men can be found. They keep themselves acquainted with neighborhood affairs, knowing only as much of what is going on in the world as can be gathered from a weekly newspaper, carelessly read; by force of necessity made acquainted with some art of livelihood, they devote every energy to making money. This occupies all their thoughts, shapes all their plans, and engrosses what dull capacity of feeling they have. Everywhere one can run against such men; they abound in all thoroughfares. It is sometimes curious to stop and study to see to what a small measure a man may be dwarfed, and to what dull stolidity he may be reduced.

Till, better than such, one has some apprehension of the reach possible to human thought, has sounded the depths of his heart, felt the bitterness of sin, longed to be free from its curse, and has looked with the anxiety of a personal concern into the possibilities of the future; till then, he feels no need of a God; and whatever his creed, lives in practical disbelief of God's personal sovereignty. That with such the Kingdom of Evil should be a success, need be no matter of debate or wonder.

There is another class of men equally determined in their disbelief of a personal God. They are not men of dull thought and sluggish feelings, but of strong and deep passions. Some passion has gained mastery over them, and holds them in complete subjection. They comprehend clearly the situation. They see that, if there be at the head of affairs in this universe a Divine and Holy Sovereign, as they sometimes fear, then the passion to whose indulgence they have sold themselves, is forbidden by his law, and must in the end incur its penalty, which means utter and eternal ruin. What course they will take is a question which often comes up, sometimes when they are not troubled with any deep sense of its consequences, sometimes when passion rages, fascinating them with the pleasure of indulgence, when the lure easily ensnares them. But even when a more thoughtful time comes, with its clearer view of the peril of indulgence, and with a more decisive utterance of conscience, then habit comes in with its reinforcement, and passion again gets ascendency.

Disturbed by perhaps a traditional belief in a personal God and by remorse of conscience, the delight of their passional enjoyments is marred. The belief or even thought of such a God sternly forbidding their passional indulgence, prolongs and makes terrible the conflict. This cannot be endured; will not be, long. But passion will not cease its clamor; so belief in such a God is questioned, debated, doubted, and finally denied, though not without many misgivings. This may not be by any formal and self-conscious process. The deceived heart keeps in concealment the weak logic of reaching such a conclusion. It is a conscious self-deception, that will not bear scrutiny for fear of exposure. No candid inquiry is instituted, no arguments examined, no one of all the weighty reasons for believing in God are set aside, no clear and candid judgment is obtained; but counsel is taken of passion; and as in olden time, the miserable "fool sayeth in his heart, there is no God."

Of all deniers of a personal God, this class is, perhaps, the largest. Men deny this doctrine, — a doctrine first, not less in philosophy than in religion; few by any honestly instituted inquiry and rigid process of ratiocination; more because, dull of thought, they have not appreciated the reasons that have carried conviction to the best minds of the race; some because so torpid in their sensibilities that they have no apprehension of the deep wants of the heart, which God only can meet; most because driven by some passion, some impulse of ambition, or greed of gain, from which they will not be persuaded, and which they cannot follow in their way, while holding a practical belief in God. These are the godless men, met day by day. They peremptorily refuse a belief that would check them in their chosen way.

What support these give to the Kingdom of Evil needs no elaborate showing. Every one, making such denial, whether by formal arguments or by unexamined impulse of heart, belongs to the Kingdom of Evil, and counts in that vast number whose multitude makes the success of that Kingdom. Of such character and in such vast numbers, whatever else they bring to that Kingdom, they give it an outward, visible, and numerical success.

CHAPTER XVI.

FURY OF THE PASSIONS.

WERE the passions of human nature modest in their demeanor and moderate in their incentives, they would be only a weak force in the Kingdom of Evil. Such signs of weakness would invite attack and secure overthrow. Of a different sort are the passions that have the handling of men. There is a violence and fury in them so imperious and impetuous, that they drive men headlong to ruin. They stand round about the Kingdom of Evil, like an invincible guard, to bar any escape. They pervade all lengths and breadths of that Kingdom with their machinations, and by ruthlessly dominating over men, become an element of success.

The imperiousness of their rule, their terrible fury, and the dominion which thereby the Kingdom of Evil gets over men, can be fitly set forth in no general terms. The practical working of one passion after another must be taken up, to see the elements of success they are to the Kingdom of Evil. In the limits assigned, the entire family of the passions cannot be depicted, nor a full portraiture be drawn of any. Only a few of the more destructive will be presented; and in this we turn from what they might be supposed, from the nature of the case, to do in their moderate or intense action, to a simple inquiry for fact. How in actual life do these passions handle men?

Take that prevalent and familiar passion, drunkenness. Let one recall what he has seen of its violence, witnessed of its fury, or the more he has read of its destructiveness upon all that is necessary to complete manhood and integrity of soul. So destructive in its ravage, that we are at no loss for facts; so prevalent, that we know not where to begin. Not even all its specimen varieties can be presented in our limits.

Taken in its beginning and in moderate power, it leads a young man into carousal. The next morning his physical wretchedness, and the sense of shame for the fool he has made of himself, lead him, if not to forswear all further indulgence, at least to a fixed purpose of holding it in moderation. Alas, poor fellow! he knows not the spirit and resources of the foe he has encountered. To other and more degrading indulgences is he led, as if the demon, intemperance, had a hook in his nose. Then his shame becomes more poignant and his resolves more vigorous, but as vain. A sense of danger may be aroused. He may set himself about to be an outcast from the fellowship of associates, to fall short of all the noble ambitions of manhood, to have his name bandied about as a drunken sot, to be left to herd with the lowest and vilest, and to get the wild and ruinous delirium of intoxication in exchange for the rational joys of life,—no matter, there is fury enough in drunkenness to compel all that, despite his weak protest or purpose.

Take now a man who has mortgaged himself to all manly ways by the responsibilities of domestic relations. His wife's alarm and his children's shame at first discovery of his intoxication, rein him up to an attitude of defence against this foe. He would hide it from his children, and protests to his wife that never again will he go to such lengths. But moderate drinking takes the key-stone from the arch on which his hopes rest, and out of the ruin he staggers a drunken man. He sees business neglected, property slipping away, prosperity gone, home cheerless and desolate, himself sinking lower in the esteem of others and in conscious degradation; his wife as sad as the destruction of all her fond hopes could make her, that keener anguish may enter his soul; his children ashamed of him, so that they would gladly disown him. All this may be, not for a day, but gathering force and intensity through long years of sorrow, of seen and felt ruin; and the future gives promise of nothing better, of no change but for the worse; and yet, vow and writhe and struggle as he will, drunkenness with imperious rule holds him firmly in its grasp.

Intemperance has tried its hand with a man still better fortified. In addition to domestic ties, he may be honored with public trusts. Responsible duties of office, pledged faith to constituents, and all schemes of political ambition may bid him break loose from the hold of intemperance; this may be demanded by an indignant constituency and promised in the hearing of the nation; but what cares the demon of intemperance for that? It can march him into most public places, into halls of Congress, and there, in sight of all the people and representatives of other nations, compel him to make a fool of himself, degrade his name, shame his constituents, and pollute his office.

The demon of intemperance has taken in hand men of genius and culture, men of finest organization, and admired for their gifts; and from the artist's studio, the poet's study, the scholar's library, the lawyer's office, the judge's bench, the professor's chair, and the minister's pulpit, he has let the occupants down through the mire of drunkenness, to poorhouse, insane asylum, or penitentiary, and finally to a drunkard's grave. It was not easily done. Men of such gifts and culture feel degradation as no others can. Stoutly they resist, inch by inch contest the ground, arouse themselves by the sense of personal peril, stiffen themselves by their hard and well-earned repute, strengthen themselves by the trust which up-looking souls repose in them; then, turning away from personal relations, they have looked over the field of study, to the research of which they had given life, but which intemperance forbids them further to explore; and then away to Him, the God of all truth, whose light had been the sun of their intellectual world, now fading, and from their minds passing away into an envelope of perfect darkness. In horror at their condition and prospect, they cry out with anguish for deliverance, and struggle as men only can when more than life is in peril. But what of all that? Intemperance can lead them back to their cups, down to a lower degradation, only to find a lower still. What wrestlings there have been on this arena! fitly represented by the fabled priest and his sons with the enveloping serpents, by those struggles adequately represented only in their fatal termination. Before the utmost fury of this passion, how feeble the resistance of a merely human force!

Then, as if to show how wanton and reckless it could be in the expenditure of its power, intemperance has taken hold of woman, endowed with rare gifts and high culture, guarded by all defences of civilization outwardly and refinement inwardly, made stronger still by her repugnance to animalism, her quick sense of propriety and purity, and her high spiritual tone. But like any cheapest woman, she must come to the low level to which intemperance beckons her. The contest that thrills her delicate organism wastes too furiously to be long. Sharp and decisive is the battle. She cannot consent to abdicate her womanhood, to be disrobed of her purity, to be clothed in shame, to be brought as low and made as vile as humanity can be; but the demon of intemperance can goad her on, and crush her down to a level as much lower as before she was higher. Let such a passion rage and raven and ravage, and the Kingdom of Evil need not despair of success.

And its prevalence harmonizes well with its power. Its statistics are frightful to one coming freshly to a knowledge of them. It alone would seem an adequate motor-power in the Kingdom of Evil. Its success is made sure in the spirit, principles, and number of those who are under the power of intemperance, toying with it, or engaged in promoting it.

But if drunkenness be king of passions, it has its court and a large retinue of attendants. Lust, debauchery, profanity, recklessness, idleness, and the long list of spendthrift and corrupting vices come in its train. These organized forces and strong defences of that Kingdom are in all parts of the land. Wherever habitations become numerous and society dense enough to fester any corruption, there the working of this passion and these attendant vices are found, destroying all that is fair and of good repute in society. When a trans-continental railroad opens new and vast regions to settlement, grog-shops, hells of gambling and harlotry are in advance of the church and school-house. There is enterprise as well as success in the Kingdom of Evil.

But intemperance is not alone. There is fury in lust. It involves the loss of all that makes life desirable, brings shame, vilest degradation, induces most horrible disease, holds in its brief future whatever human hearts can dread, and brings the grave within reach of a few years, to say nothing of what lies beyond. And yet its fury drives on rough-shod. It may involve perfidy to the most sacred entrustment man ever received from woman, plighted love, the charge of a trustful soul, the safe-keeping of the heart's happiness. All these it can dash down into remediless ruin. The honor implied, when she temporarily entrusted her person to his safe-keeping for a walk or a ride, goes for nothing. False vows may gain his end; but if not, if there be opposed the indignation of offended modesty, tender pleadings, such beseeching as only greatest peril calls out, and she resist by force to the last endurance, — the fury of lust can break down all resistance, deterred by not one of the terrible things that must follow. And to get rid of the least of these, he has smitten his victim down in death, that she may not tell of his guilt. From abroad the land, often is the fact of such outrage brought to us in the chronicle of the press.

Not merely thus impetuous is the fury of this passion. It can be cool and deliberate, if that be the price of gratification. Introduction, acquaintance, intimacy, friendship, love, plighted faith, solemnest vows, are approaches that may have taken months, only to gain the power to ruin. And if that ruin involve the bedimming of a gem, the fall of a star from heaven, a life of anguish, and to a wide circle such sorrow as death never brought, the fury of this lust is competent to all that.

It can approach a woman consecrated to another at the altar of marriage. With siren voice it can charm her silly ear, fill some of the vacancies in her heart with distrust of her husband, offer grateful pity for imagined wrongs, pave the way by fondling, seduce the heart, and then pollute the person. It may involve the separation of husband and wife, the ruin of a family, liability to legal arrest, or greater liability to a husband's vengeance: no matter; the fury of this passion takes no account of risks or vengeance or guilt. What years of anguish follow, it stops not to count. Just such fury is there in this lust, which enters so many hearts as to be an element of success in the Kingdom of Evil.

The fury of passion is seen in the retaliative blow of hot anger or deliberate revenge. Incensed by wrong, real or imagined, how quick such blows have come, how fatal they have been. Hot dispute over, it may be, a trifle; differences which a few calm words could have adjusted, have stirred quick resent and nerved murderous blows: the whole within the limit of an hour; the guilt, if not remorse, to darken all the rest of life.

In former times it curbed itself to the regulation of the duelling code, nursing itself to the strength and intensity of more deliberate vengeance. If before such fury former friend fall, a wife be written widow, and children fatherless; if penalty of civil law be incurred, or the slayer wander forth under the stigma of Cain, — no matter; vengeance takes no account of consequences. When its fury has been spent and its victim smitten down in death, how terrible the stroke of remorse that comes. The duellist has dropped his murderous pistol, rushed to his victim, implored life to stay, and sought to stanch the blood his vengeance made flow. Poignant regret, bitter remorse, self-cursing, are of no avail now. These, passion in its blind fury refused to see. It saw nothing but vengeance, quick and fell.

But if hot anger and quick blows must not be, the fury of hate can be cool and calculating; can forecast a plan of vengeance and take time — sometimes years — for its execution. Stealthily the net is spread. He entices his victim into the snare, even by cajolement if necessary. The gratification of his imperious hate is the central purpose of his current life; that it is by means so terrible as murder, only gives the business an importance that fills his thoughts and taxes his powers. To compass this murder, he makes every other purpose subordinate and every plan subservient. Fear of consequences to himself, the possibility of detection, and the penalty of the law make him pause, perhaps exhibit such eccentricities as to entitle him, upon arrest, to the plea of insanity; but his unrelenting hate will not stop. He nerves it to greater strength by recount of his wrongs and their aggravation. Then he reviews his scheme of revenge, charges his prudence to make it sure that every step be covered up, and every clew to discovery be hidden; as if, with so great a disturbance in mind, he could preserve his powers in balance, forecast all the exigencies that might arise, or bring nature into league with his crime.

Then, when the deed is done and vengeance spent, he trembles at his guilt and holds himself to the imperious duty of concealing it. Even his assumed naturalness seems awkward; he chides his mental disquietude, fearing lest the conduct it prompts and the look it gives, will show his guilt. Then when he remembers that gases will float the body to the surface, that fire will not consume bones, that blood stains so deeply, and that human blood will not be confounded with any other; already he feels the grasp of arrest and hears the verdict — "Guilty, as charged in the indictment." But the fury of hate and revenge can blind his fears again.

Through the years and to-day such vengeful hate festers in some hearts, such schemes of murder brew. The daily papers report them as accomplished. If the success of the Kingdom of Evil is helped by crimes, clearly there are in human nature passions so furious and crimes so fearful as to leave that success in no dispute.

Another passion that has fury in it, is gambling. The excitement of risk has a fascination; there is curiosity to know how things will turn. When this is enhanced by hope of gain and fear of loss, another element of intensity is added. But the game also affords some play for skill. Delicacy of touch, steadiness of nerve, certainty of aim, balance of mind, quickness of calculation, and tenacity of memory, are of use, may be put to utmost task. When these powers have been so drilled as to give easy mastery over presuming novices, plucking them readily, then the gambler will match himself with others of like skill. Then come into play the excitement of risk, prospect of heavy gain or loss, and the contest of rivalship in skill, which, in certain lines, tax human powers to their utmost. In these lie the overmastering fury of this passion.

And such is this fury, that men have exposed to the risks of gambling, not simply funds which they could safely withdraw from business, but their necessary capital, stock in trade, real estate, all laboriously-gained earnings, their last dollar, necessaries for family comfort and decency, and then the garments on their own persons. And then, reduced to beggary, with not a dollar more of cash or credit, by suicide they have gone from the gambler's hell to another.

Even so terrible a passion has a side worthy only of ridicule, as has all sin because of its essential manners. Let the young men of a city or village, too stupid to be brilliant in anything, whose gayety is only boisterousness, who get out of their dulness of thought and feeling only when half drunk, meet to gamble as well as they know how; and in their bets, in their awkward playing and disputes about it, the flatness of the whole affair, like stupid men playing dominos, — almost too silly to be wicked,— is so worthy only of ridicule, that, were this all, little would need be said against gambling.

But gambling takes on forms worthy of such repute as fashion gives. The large amounts of money that pass from hand to hand, the magnificence of the hall in which its deeds are done, the splendor of the rooms in which its ruins are wrought, the intensity of mental action brought into play, — rather put to work, men so cool and even complaisant without, yet having such heats within, — the ruin of fortune and the wreck of moral character show both the respectability and the fury of this passion, and as well how it helps the Kingdom of Evil to success.

Another passion whose fury enlists for the success of the Kingdom of Evil, is Ambition. What schemes of conquest it has pushed, what wars of subjugation it has carried on, what thrones it has overturned, what nationalities it has blotted out, for what long ages it has held back civilization and the gospel, the history and condition of many countries can testify.

To such exercise of this passion many are not prone, or had they gifts equal thereto, the lack of opportunity keeps them safe. But ambition has less conspicuous theatres of action. On all levels of life, it finds opportunity to brace up weak points in the Kingdom of Evil. To an ambition for position in society, persons have sacrificed all that was noble and genuine in personal character. Truth, simplicity, honor, integrity of character, and usefulness of life gone, that they may follow in the ways of fashionable folly and dissipation. To maintain a corresponding style of life, and ape the silly ways of fashion, they have incurred debts past all payment, descended to tricks and finesse that would shame an honest man. That such short-lived folly must run a speedy race and come to an ignominious fall, checks not its fury. Elegant mansions dot the land, which over-ambitious builders have been compelled to vacate, leaving them to men of better prudence, and leaving them to stand as monuments of their foolish ambition. Every such illustration of ambitious pride and folly helps the Kingdom of Evil.

Saddest instances are to be found in matters of less conspicuousness. Ambition for dress and finery takes possession of a woman's mind. Such ambition, if gratified, gives no proof of personal virtues or noble qualities of mind, as the richly-attired harlot shows; clearly it is not to gratify a pure taste, for that involves simplicity and fitness to condition. Yet instances abound, in which women, and some young men, expend all they can earn in the adornment of their persons. No fear of coming want, or any best use of money, can divert a dollar from outward adornment. The greed of this passion sometimes exceeds the earnings of industry. When credit fails, women have taken to shop-lifting. And such ascendency has this passion gained over some, that, married or unmarried, they have prostituted their own persons to gain the means of adorning them; no matter how vile inwardly, if only gay in outward adornment. So they help the Kingdom of Evil to success.

One other passion deserves mention for its fury, Avarice. There is method in its madness. It has reasons. The future is so pregnant with wants; these may be so many and urgent, that their unknown possibilities appall the mind. These wants, in the shape they take to many minds, can be met with money.

This passion will lead men to deny themselves any rational enjoyment of life, to refuse their children the mental food furnished by books, papers, magazines, music, and art; to deny them adequate education and any knowledge of the world by travel; some to refuse their children a fair chance to hear the gospel. Manifold are the starvations which avarice imposes. Then to what perils it will lead men to subject themselves. Many are found broken down in middle life by tasks avarice laid on them.

In distant regions, in unknown lands, in sickness away from relief, in dangerous employments, in storm, in flood, in peril of starvation, in liability to accident, death is braved. Men will go to death's door and hell's gateway for gold. Richer, if they die for it!

Inexpressibly mean this passion can make men. Some will sell any friendship, if retaining costs money or losing it brings gain; fail in all the kindly relations and gracious offices of social life; subject themselves to the contempt of all rightly-acting minds,— the sentence must stand incomplete, for language fails to express the unqualified meanness of an avaricious, miserly man.

How wicked this passion can make men, the world knows too well. Men will lie, cheat, steal, rob, murder, and ruin soul as well as body, to make money. How many would laugh one in the face, if he assigned the wickedness of their course as a reason for giving up their successful way of making money. Human ingenuity may be taxed to contrive an act so wicked that some men will not be willing to make money thereby; and of which all would say, — evidently profitable, but too wicked. If profitable, it will be adopted, though as wicked as possible. Such is the fury of Avarice, as history has shown, and as is seen to-day.

Not one can deny the fact of these passions, nor their fury. It befits sin to show itself thus. Such malignant forces are in the very genius of sin. So they are at work in society, one here and another there, swelling and festering human hearts to an extent sometimes reputable, sometimes disreputable, destroying peace, sullying repute, damaging temporal welfare, degrading the soul from its true level, forbidding it a normal life, and constructing a past which can issue only in ruin eternal and remediless. These passions in their fury induce iniquities, vices, crimes, and guilt; and these are capital and power in the Kingdom of Evil.

Besides, they raise the average temperature of passions throughout society. They create an atmosphere of evil which every man must breathe. No man can disown his surroundings and keep himself from their influence. The enormous wickedness which these passions daily perpetrate augment the moral distemperature of society. The known working of these terrible and furious passions countenance their repetition, encourage more modest passions and less pretentious iniquities. Thereby they become a fruitful element of success in the Kingdom of Evil.

CHAPTER XVII.

THE POWER OF TALK.

THAT of which the heart is fullest is sometimes kept closest. Love may give the heart its quickest throbs, and the tongue refuse to speak of it, even to most intimate friends. It may take fullest possession of every thought and feeling; may be an ever-present gladness and give hues of brightness to all aspects of the future, and yet the lips refuse to whisper it, even in secret. So, some scheme of ambition, pleasure, wealth, study, or usefulness may occupy the waking thoughts and give shape to dreams, not for brief times, but for months and years; yet, while in design and awaiting full maturity, the tongue may speak of anything more freely than of that.

This, however, is illustrated only by those who have command of their lips and mastery of their tongues. Some are incontinent, and cannot hold anything capable of utterance in words. If anything be in them, it must come out by leakage at the mouth. They will talk, even when they have nothing to say. Others are unnaturally and provokingly reticent,— Yes and No their main utterances. They have this show of wisdom; they are choice in their words.

Talk and thought are often in such disproportion as paper money bears to specie, — ruinous inflation, redeemable at very low percentage. The words of some are worth their face; others, not the air it took to give them articulation.

The world is very outspoken, and there is meaning in its talk. What is the world talking about? At its places of concourse and along its ways of travel is heard a ceaseless babble of talk, and in earnest tones; but on what themes? It will raise no dispute to affirm that the great burden of all this talk is worldliness. What should the world do but talk of its own affairs? Not long will one listen to a knot of men without hearing the words, dollar, per cent. Modes of investment, kinds of business, the crops, state of the markets, plans of work, prospects of gain, schemes of pleasure, tokens of success or failure, all the manifold shapes and aspects these can take are talked over exhaustively and exhaustingly. The news, the weather, accidents, the war, improvements going on, the fashions current and coming, the last wedding and the next, — how naturally these are taken up by most tongues.

The world's newspapers show the drift of its talk. News from abroad, posture of contending armies, attitude of surrounding nations, price of gold and grain, acts of congress and cabinet, elections held or in prospect, excursions, curiosities of the census, fires, murders, robberies, divorces, confidence games, races, storms, floods, all these goings-on get into the papers, because these are what men want to read about and then talk about. Secular papers contain religious news, because they must keep up with the times, and tell what is going on. A missionary convention gets reported, and a murder trial, for the same reason. Vice sometimes gets rebuked, and common moralities secure advocacy. This may be grateful to the conductors of the press, or may not. If demanded by the Christianized state of society, the press can be valiant for righteousness. Yet even this, and putting the telegraph to religious uses, is counted by many as an impertinence; as though sin had a pre-empted right to all ways of utterance.

Hush all the babble of sin, stop the world's talk about schemes of worldliness, its cry for gain, clamor for passion, gossip of fashion, and all personal detraction, and what silence there would be! Could all the profanity, grumbling, and indecent talk be hushed, the world would be much quieter than now.

The style of the world's talk make it an element of success in the Kingdom of Evil. In places of business, on the street, at home, around the table, in the parlor, the style of talk indulged is such as one might expect, if it were known, as past all doubt, that the world and its inhabitants were to continue as now for ages. If it would take a thousand years for the men of this generation to find their graves, if beyond the grave there was nothing that could arouse a fear or excite a hope, the present non-religious or anti-religious style of the world's talk would not excite surprise.

But beyond dispute, or doubt of any sane mind, there is coming in the history of each one a most revolutionary experience; an absolute separation from all the business, relations, and affinities of this life; an entrance upon a condition as different, possibly as much better, or as much worse, as the human mind can conceive. Take those who count this true, and living on intimate terms with them for months and years, we find not in their conversation the remotest allusion to the most stupendous certainty awaiting them. Does not this raise a doubt of the sincerity of their faith, or the sanity of their minds?

All men know that the transformation of death awaits them, that that transformation will cut them off from all the business, relations, and affinities of life, and that, separated from the body, they will be ushered into very different conditions of life. To this aspect of the future no sane mind presents a denial or doubt. Positively to deny or sincerely to doubt the fact of death and the transformation it works in the conditions of existence, would excite the derision we feel for folly, or the pity we have for insanity.

Yet to such folly, if not insanity, the drift of the world's talk carries men. If all the inhabitants of the land had met in convention to determine how most effectually to banish from their minds the fact of their mortality and the Godward relations of the soul, so that these should have no power in directing thought, giving tone to feeling, or shape to conduct; by no method could it have been so surely as by inaugurating the present style of the world's talk. If this illusion be broken up by the death of one of their fellows, they accept the fact, since they must, and hush briefly, or sink to quieter tone their worldly talk; but as soon as they can give him burial, thought, feeling, and the talk thereby diverted swing back into former forgetfulness of such an event as awaiting them in the near-by future. No repetitions can bring them to a truer view of life, or break the strange spell under which they live.

What holds them in a position justified only by folly or insanity? If not done, it is helped by the world's talk. Ceaselessly it calls attention to this scheme of worldliness, or that method of gain; to this enterprise of ambition, or that plan of pleasure; holding the mind to a vision so restricted that death in the background is not seen. It is as if each had bound themselves to banish all thought of dying and of the soul's Godward relations from their own and every other mind.

The level to which the world's talk holds the mind gives it no range which takes in God, immortality, salvation, or any other great reality of religion. This general announcement, though received without dispute, fails to carry to the mind the terrible fact it contains. It will take some hard thinking, truly, to conceive how terribly the mind is wronged by being shut up in such seclusion. To be cut off from the things with which it has mainly to do; shut away from the avenues through which its highest dignity and welfare can be reached; kept from that range of thought in which alone its highest powers and richest gifts find exercise; shut away from those supplies which only can meet its ineradicable wants; to unsphere the soul and let it rush to ruin; to keep the soul from the best it can be, from the highest it can reach, and the richest it can enjoy, — this is what is done; out of all this the soul is talked by the world's talk.

Go where one will, into homes, on the streets, along thoroughfares of travel, in cars, steamers, hotels, fashionable watering-places, through marts of trade, social circles, and to the very doors of the sanctuary and what will he hear save the babble of worldliness, sinking oftener to profanity and obscenity, than rising to any grasp of the highest and grandest things with which the mind has to do? All this is around every soul like a mephitic atmosphere, an inbreathed pestilence, palsying the powers and narrowing the range of thought, also benumbing the sensibilities of the heart.

The world's talk is possessed of the devil, never demoniac more so. Had Satan put his ingenuity to contriving a way of making the world's talk an element of success in the Kingdom of Evil, how could it have been done better than now? And of this we would be the more deeply impressed, could we pass from the general character and pervasive power of the world's talk to a detailed consideration of its different forms. If we could take up for examination the main elements of the world's talk, the greedy avarice, the restless ambition, the low animalism, the daring profanity, the prurient obscenity, the ill-concealed falsehoods, the incitements to lawless pleasure, the stinging scorn, the vengeful hate, the spirit of caste, the benumbing hilarity, the reckless indifference to life's sober realities, all of which find large occupancy in the world's talk,—not only see these, but also their effects on certain temperaments, proclivities, and conditions of mind; could we thus stop and examine minutely what is going on through sway of the world's talk, we should have a more impressive sense of the element of success it is in the Kingdom of Evil.

Many a sceptical argument has put away all fear of God from the minds of young men; advocacy of pleasure and appeals to pride, with the deceit of flatteries, have opened the way of ruin to many a young woman: obscene stories have tainted many a mind with corruption; tricks of gain and crafty success, told to those ambitious for wealth, fostered their mammonism and incited them to lawless ways of gain. The more we look into its details, the more obviously an element of success in the Kingdom of Evil will the world's talk be found.

The great bulk of talk with some religious people is on the same level, its voice in the same key. They are not less men for being Christians. They have the same wants, responsibilities, and work as other men. Living in a physical body, they must give it heed, lay their plans, push their industries, enter into competition, hold their place, and make room for themselves in the world's affairs. They cannot do this in dumb silence. So, much of their talk must be like that of any sensible man of the world. None have a better right to such use of their tongues. It matters not what position they hold in the church, they cannot abdicate their manhood, nor resign its responsibilities. They must eat and drink, be clothed and housed, must love, and provide for their loved ones. For this they must be in the world's work and the world's talk. To what deeper significance and higher level this talk may reach with cultivated Christians, will be considered further on.

Into this necessary talk on life's affairs, some cannot adjust religious conversation naturally, gracefully, nor comfortably. Their uncultivated and unharmonized consciences are often troubled by the almost unbroken worldliness of their talk. They make an awkward dash out of it into what they count religious conversation, sometimes by adopting the phrases of religious cant, as profitless as the worldliest talk. They have no idea of fitness or graceful turns in conversation, and so lug in religion by main force, in violation of all laws governing association of thought. To such, nothing is religious conversation that does not include an examination into the orthodoxy of one's creed, or the moralities of his life. So they put him into the confessional, subject him to examination and cross-examination, tear open, if they can, all secrets of heart and life, and would be best satisfied had they some chemical power of analyzing the moral constituents of the soul. Like rebel surgeons amputating the limbs of Federal soldiers, they care nothing for suffering or consequences; they want to exercise their gifts, and their tongues give sorer wounds than surgeon's knife. Their minds are too coarse to detect the religious brutality they inflict. Their tongues sting as suddenly and hurtfully as a scorpion's. Here and there society is infested with these religious wasps, and happy is he who can escape their sting.

Offsetting these are the cowardly deferential. They have an egregious sense of proprieties. They never turn conversation into a religious channel without offering an apology for it, — generally needful for their awkward way of doing it. They seldom offend, prevented by their enormous modesty. They see a Christian brother in peril, evidently infatuated with some worldly ambition, some appetite or lust, — the proprieties of his Christian walk and the stabilities of his moral character giving way without his seeming to know it. A faithful, tender, loving statement of the case to him, presenting this fact and that truth to quicken conscience, arouse fear, excite hope, and to gird up his laxities with Christian firmness, would save that soul from devious wandering and the church from disrepute. But such faithfulness is too much for their weak modesty; so they suffer sin upon a brother, and there come years of backsliding that might have been saved by an hour's Christian talk.

Of the two classes outlined, not fully portrayed, the first disturb the current of the world's talk only to make it muddier; the other lets it flow on, however lethean or tumultuously destructive it may be, and neither hinder the world's talk from helping the Kingdom of Evil to success.

Unwilling to be shut up to this, one may inquire: How can he guide his way amid these currents and counter-currents of talk, so as to gain some straightforwardness and dignified use of speech? His feeling is not to help the Kingdom of Evil by the use of a sentence or syllable. How not to do this?

The end is within reach, yet under no single and simple rule. He will have to participate in a great deal of just such talk as the men of the world use. He may keep it clean from the foulness which the evil mix into their talk; may keep his speech far above the profanity, obscenity, mammonism, frothy hilarity, vapid jocoseness, and personal detraction which enter so largely into the world's talk; but while he is in the body, he must have a hand in the world's business and a share in its talk. He must breathe the air that is around him, though not the purest. Yet this does not deny him the right of using disinfectants. The protest of silence or of open rebuke may afford him the only escape from helping the Kingdom of Evil.

So far as he participates in the world's talk, he will quite likely be misunderstood. The range of speech covers a broad zone. He may be well up in it, others low down, while many cannot see the difference. Some have never found out the different meanings the same sentence may have. These are beyond the detection of grammar or rhetoric; no analysis of the words can reach them. One recites the simplest fact after his morning salutation to a neighbor; for example, that a violent storm raged during the night; assenting, both are counted as having said the same thing. It looks like simple and easy talk on level of worldly affairs; this and nothing more. Yet though both met in using the same sentence, their minds could not be much further apart.

In it the one saw damage to his crops, delay of work, disruption of plans, and curtailment of profit. The sentence uttered finds his mind drifting in a sea of worldliness, buffeting waves of selfishness, and grumbling at God's appointments of weather. The mind of the other approaches the fact mentioned on another side entirely. In using that sentence he saw nature refreshed, the air purified, conditions created more favorable to health, and the sentence stirs his heart with gratitude to a Heavenly Father.

At the next turn of the conversation the sickness of a neighbor may be mentioned. That sentence tells one of work not done, or likely to be; of payments not made, and of losses thereby incurred. Such are the meanings with which that sentence is freighted to his mind. His thoughts move on a level which takes in a view of affairs that is worldly without mitigation. The mind of the other in the sentence used finds a very different meaning: he sees a soul trembling on the verge of another world, hunting after evidences of salvation; repentance renewing its work, faith clinging to Christ, and a family standing under the shadow of a great sorrow. With all these that sentence comes laden to his mind; a simple sentence, yet bearing to two minds meanings and a train of thoughts so different.

So we may run through all admissible talk about the world's affairs; and from mention made of any object of nature, of national, historical, personal, phenomenal, political, commercial, criminal, social, and other affairs, persons may meet in using the same sentence; but it is like the point of juncture between two spheres, — their thoughts are in orbits entirely different. To one it is worldly talk, having no other meaning; to the other it has been eminently religious. On such different levels minds live, which nevertheless touch each other in that broad zone which bounds talk on this world's affairs. To one it is simple worldliness, without remotest recognition of anything beyond gain or pleasure. To the other, all this world's affairs, thus talked about, stand related, as really they are, to God, soul-discipline, and the eternal issues of life. Such different meanings have Christian and worldly talk on a common theme, and even in using the same sentence.

The conversation of every thoughtful Christian, let it begin where it will, tends inward and upward. From bleakest fact, most ordinary event, and worldliest subject, there is a natural and ready approach to matters which interest the soul in its highest and Godward relations. All natural turns in conversation may lead off in this direction. Under sanctified association of thought, and the open-heartedness of a truly Christian life, the drift of talk flows naturally into channels that reach the broad ocean of religious truth, whose further shores touch the climes of immortality.

A soul truly alive to the grandest things of life, quickened by the inspirations of the gospel, runs through all talk of most outward affairs a vein of religious thought and feeling, ready at fit turns in conversation to flow forth in expression; just as we might expect of one living in fellowship with the Father and the Son, and, as his hopes hold him, on the verge of heaven. But shut all this away; hide from thought life's grandest realities; let the soul be blinded to its noblest capacities and highest relations, and all talk on this world's affairs will be the worldliest possible, — barren, shallow, as wellnigh meaningless as possible, even though having in use the moulds, forms, and images of the highest truths.

Such is the world's talk, — tethered to material things, reaching to no depth of the heart's meaning, to no height of the soul's aspirations, dealing in platitudes that give the thoughts no inspiration. Trivial and shallow are the things which custom lets the world talk about. Religious thought finds scant welcome; even when talk runs dry, awkwardest silence rather than this. Holding minds to such narrow range, upon such low levels, shutting them away from inmost and deepest things of life, away from the Infinite and Eternal, which only can meet the soul's wants and powers, the world's talk, ceaselessly doing this, can be only an element of success in the Kingdom of Evil.

CHAPTER XVIII.

LEVELS REACHED OR NOT.

SOME live in a level country, where in no direction they can see farther than to the fringe of forests that girdle them round on every side. These lie within a mile or two; beyond, they see only the clouds or the sky. Tame ocean view would bring the relief of giving the eye a wider sweep. On all sides the sky shuts down close around, and the horizon in all its circumference measures less than a dozen miles.

The rest of the township lies out of sight. Only a few farms in the county come under range of vision. The State spreads out all around, as the geography tells, but the eye cannot see the amplitude of its territory. Farther on, what sweeps of continent there are, reaching from ocean to ocean, from the perpetual verdure of the tropics to the everlasting snows of polar regions. If imagination can reach so far, the eye can follow only a mile or two. The trees standing there hide all beyond. By read ing or travel it may not be a *terra incognita*, but is a *terra occulta*.

We sometimes chafe at this restricted vision. It

stifles us. The small, tiresome, and almost changeless picture, seen three hundred and sixty-five days every year, becomes a blank to the wearied eye. If some one builds a new house, one good that comes of it is, that it gives variety to the dull picture. It would be a relief if some houses and barns would burn up; but as this would not be convenient to the owners, to change the scene and get larger vision, one can almost master his timidity enough to go up in a balloon at the risk of his precious neck.

There are other conditions of life. To some it is a relief to be buried far down in a valley, into which the sun does not peep till a late hour of the morning, early in the afternoon hiding from sight behind a mountain range, though long before sunset; on the lofty sides and high battlements of the opposite mountain they see his sheen slowly retreating to the mountain-top, accessible to nothing else, save the winds and snows. They have something distant to look at, something beyond reach, a step towards the Infinite.

But there is something better than this. We can climb the mountains. Going up the hill-side windings, we come to outlooks whence the circle in which before we lived, and which bounds our earthly interests, looks scarcely bigger than a garden. Higher up we go, finding how much larger is the earth than the world in which we lived. Winding around the mountain-sides, the vista, on this hand and that, opens in wider perspective. Here and there — not less than a dozen of them — are villages. We see the shimmer of their white and the outlines of their church spires. Farther away can be seen the smoke of the city. The thread of river and mirror of lake are distinctly marked, and the varieties of green and brown and blue add beauty to the picture.

Going to greater heights, we pass the region of clouds, and for a while look off only on billows of fog. Their contortions and heavings tell us that the wind has taken them in hand, is dashing cloud against cloud, and far below our unbroken sunshine is drenching the earth with rain. The elemental strife soon ceases; the clouds tumble about and float away; and then to the eye comes a vision of grandeur and beauty. On beyond the villages we had counted, and the lakes beyond hill and valley, rise the mountains, one behind another, in the blue distance; while at one side of the range, and farther on, we see the ocean and catch the flash of its waves.

One comes down from that mountain-top a wiser man. The earth has grown in his respect. It reaches farther than his fancy had gone. Life is more to him than before. He feels stimulated to an endeavor and conscious of a power that never stirred him before. On that mountain-top, life and all things have met a transfiguration.

There is more varied scenery than such topography presents; deeper valleys, higher mountains, more restricted and ampler vision. Life has levels, ranges, outlooks, and reaches of perspective more various than earth's surface presents. Differences between men, in the range of their thoughts and in the scope of their aims, reach so far away towards the Infinite, as to be beyond ordinary comprehension.

It is difficult to tell how cheap and coarse the food on which the vitality and apparent health of the body can be maintained; more difficult to tell how restricted the range of thought, how cold and low-graded the impulses, that shall keep the mind in action apparently healthy. Doomed to solitary confinement during life, if through some small loop-hole he could have watch of a few rods of street, it might save a man's mind from idiocy. So little as could thus be gathered, constitutes the mental food on which some are nourished, with scarcely no relish given it by any condiment of domestic affection. And grown up to such stature of manhood as they have been able to reach, at street corners, under hotel porch, with others of like powers, in gossip of neighborhood affairs, or in stories kept from being vapid even to their own dull minds only by being salacious, they find the highest reach of their thinking and the highest elevation of their social life. Books and papers such as "Dime Novels," "Police Gazettes," and love-story magazines, come to them with exciting relish and refreshment. On so low a level are some, that they find a quickening in that style of literature.

The low levels of thought and feeling on which so many live help the Kingdom of Evil to success. Numerically, the largest portion of the adherents of that Kingdom live on such low levels and within such restrictions, that they get no outlook upon the realities around them. Their horizon shuts down close around. They see to the line of surrounding forests. Within is the world of their life; beyond is, to them, the unknown. Within such restrictions, they are likely to remain in the Kingdom of Evil.

It is worth while to come to some just notions of the restrictions under which some live. Let any one recall the men of the world whom he knows best, the style of their conversation, the topics in talking about which they seem to have the freest play of their powers and to do themselves most credit. What will be found their range of themes? The weather, the crops, under-draining, politics, current news, trade, investments, improvements, and all the varieties of secular interests; these are not indifferent affairs, of which they make mention incidentally. On these topics they find their highest elevation of thought. Here they know the most and come to the best display of their powers. If here they cannot give entertainment and win respect, they must fail of it. The white day in their year is the county fair, or some occasion in which the materialities of nature are the topics of chief interest. Beyond these they cannot see, so close around them shuts the horizon of their life.

Instead of living in such a marsh, some gain the advantage of living in a valley bounded with lofty mountains, whose peaks, so distant and far above them, seem like steps heavenward. In their seclusion from the general field of literature, science, art, philosophy, history, and theology, they have, nevertheless, taken in some one line of study, related to their calling, or towards which in some casual way they got an impulse. This line of study they follow till lost in its correlations, thereby as inaccessible as the mountain heights girding their valleys and lost in the heavenward direction. To them how much grander a thing is life, that it contains this line of study, perhaps of discovery, original, at least to them. They are on a track that leads upward, God-ward. From the hill-side windings of their path they can see afar off. They have vision of things that lie far beyond every-day interests, and the ends reached by toil and business. They get sight of things, dim and in the far distance, which meet wants of mind; things that will be in demand after death has cut the soul loose from earthly moorings. Even if by night-fall they must come back to their home in the valley, it is something, to them much, that they have been so far up the hill-side, and had an outlook reaching so far away beyond the round of every-day thoughts. They lie down at night with the conscious dignity of being more than they had thought, and dream of possibilities not reached, nor even sought before. They have had a transfiguration, even if dim and shadowy.

Just such differences there are. Some men, like herons and other waders, live along marshes, in scenes dull with fen and fog, in a dank atmosphere, which the sunshine could only make sweltering. To get their food, build their nests, and rear their young, — that is all. Others, like the eagle, soar to mountain-tops. They look far down on those wading in morasses. They see far beyond the widest vision of those who toil only for earthly good. All that the senses can get, measure, and rejoice in, lies within what they see to be only a hand-breadth of the scene covered by their vision.

In close proximity live the men whose vision has such different range. They walk the same streets, live in adjacent houses, and sit in the same sanctuary. The difference may make no show of itself in outward vocation. Alike they prosecute the industries of life, join in its amusements, meet its temporal responsibilities, and with like strictness may practise its moralities. To any judgment which the eye can form, they live about on the same level. And yet no highest mountain-top is so far above lowest morass. To the one class, life, the world, and universe, so far as they can put these to use, are for ends which every day and year demand. Beyond their earthly sojourn, and the inauguration of their children into some respectable calling, they have no thought or care. What lies outside this narrow range is nothing to them.

Is this a vilification of humanity? The appeal is made to facts lying within any one's inspection. Let him sharpen his wits and know what is going on around him. Let him gain the confidence of the most intelligent worldling within range of his acquaintance; see to what all his plans drive, what he would count success, what to him would be reasonable and richest reward. Let him sit down in a group of such men, or take any way of getting the level and range of their talk and the reach of their aims, and we submit the case to the verdict that shall be made. Meet the wants that clamor through the senses, quiet the fear that this supply may fail them in coming years, and most of them would rest in perfect content. Some of them have an ambition for some betterment; but money enough can secure that. Some have a slight uneasiness of curiosity; this can be put to rest by any intelligent and well-read man, or by waiting a few years to see how affairs will turn in this world. Such levels of society are densely populated.

Do all live in such fens and fogs? Do such quagmires overspread the world? Are there no uplands, no mountain-tops, with purer air and wider vision? It cannot be supposed that minds such as ours, capable of such reach of thought, and even of excess in feeling, should be held to the limits of such tame insipidity. Nor so is it. For all within there are objects without; color, form, and perspective, actual and possible, to delight the eye forever; melody and harmony, actual and possible, to ravish the ear perpetually; facts and truths, enough to tire the mind, could it ever tire. There is, in fulness never to be exhausted, what is worthiest of faith and trust and love. This is no desert universe. Starting on any stream, one needs only to follow it far enough to come to a fountain of infinite supply. All around lies the infinite, before the eternal. Long before one has searched out what is within reach, instead of sighing in fear of destitution, his longing will be for an eye and ear skilled by better culture; for a mind to know more accurately and comprehensively; for a heart to trust and love and adore more worthily of the occasion, and for powers adequately trained to meet the opportunity. Straightened in himself, — that 's the greatest difficulty.

Men are not all fools. Some are finding out what

is within reach in this universe, what is possible in the future, what scope there is for the soul's powers; how satisfyingly the mind can feast on truth, and how ravishingly the heart can believe, trust, love, and adore. Some have come upon the uplands; some are climbing the hill-sides. Far below lie the fens and fogs, where live the ignorant, the passionate, the brutish, and the worldly. To these upclimbing souls there is afforded so pure an air and so wide a vision, that they begin to see things in God's true perspective. They see how small and trifling are the things which buy worldly men; whose plans, occupying their thoughts; whose schemes, engrossing their hearts; whose toils, filling all the days with struggles and weariness; whose highest joys, beguiling them to ruin, are delusive, fleeting, only wave-crests, if not sooner engulfed, quickly to break on the shore. What worldlings dignify under the name of business may be overruled to contribute somewhat to the progress of society and the furtherance of God's plans; but in the design of worldly men, held simply to what they mean by it, there is not a single element in it of use or dignity, worthy of the soul's powers, relations, and opportunities; it meets only current expenses of travel through the world, in its different styles.

Christian men mean something more by it. To them, the chief value is in the training afforded to souls, and in the help it gives to humanity and the gospel. To the same uses God holds it. But take the business of the world, as worldly men hold it, in their spirit, with their aims, and for their purposes; give it all the dignity its magnitude can claim, represented in the vast amounts of its traffic, in the sums of all its investments, and in the total or all its industries; then, carry it all into the light of the eternal world and into the presence of God, and what will worldly men say it amounts to? Thus seen, it is safe to leave the estimate to their intelligence and candor.

What is fact, can be found out; what is real, can be seen true; and what is true, can be known. There are men who do not have to go through the experience of ruin to find out what is ruinous. On level with fen and enveloped in fog, some may not see far. But men have climbed up from marsh to mountain. In the pure air and wide outlook of hill-top, they look down upon the eager scrambling of worldly men, distracted even out of the dull dignity of flocks at pasture, fevered with lusts, crazed in their low ambitions, and blinded to the uses of life. Where this distraction of worldliness begins, where it will end, and what it will amount to, is visible enough; and there are men in such high outlook that they can see it.

If not actually, one can in imagination take a stand where he can look down upon worldliness in its intensest action, the seething life of a city, and watch there till a whole generation has done its work and passed away. Could he have watched with omniscient eye, have seen all that was done and kept strict account of what was accomplished by men moved only by the common impulses of worldliness, except in having such worldly enterprises overruled in the interests of the gospel and in preparing a better future for humanity, — ends not at all within their aim, — his verdict would be that that generation of men, thus watched, might as well not have been.

And just the littleness there is in their purposed aims can be seen. Myriads of clear-eyed and far-seeing Christians have the whole scope and range of worldliness directly under their vision. They are in position to see its utmost boundaries. They can say concerning it: Only this; nothing more. And as they pursue their hill-side windings, they do something more than so negative a thing as minifying worldliness. They find something positive in the range of vision which faith gives them. [No, Reader, I will not excuse you, nor admit that I am departing from the sober realities of life. I hold you to the duty of bearing me company.] For knowledge is not more normal to the human mind, nor based upon more absolute warrant, than is faith. Taking the mind in all its modes of action and moods of feeling, not more fitting and necessary to its full life and development is knowledge than faith. Not more does the soul need to know than to believe. The methods of faith are legitimate. No nicely constructed telescope is better fitted to the eye than faith to the soul. No astronomical almanac more exact than the data which faith accepts; no laws of light more exact than the laws which come into the handling of faith. More normal use is not got by the eye in seeing than by the soul in believing. The believing soul is the only soul that puts its powers to fitting use, that accepts the situation as it is, and adjusts itself into existing relations. The man that believes nothing, stands as far below his proper level as the man that knows nothing.

And souls there are, living in surrounding homes, met daily on the streets, that have such outlook as faith gives them. They have access to mountain-tops, to some Pisgah whence they can overlook the promised land. The range of their vision is telescopic. Away beyond utmost reach of worldly plans, away beyond what shrewdest men of business ever schemed, the vision of intelligent Christian faith reaches. There are men, not wiser than others in this world's affairs, perhaps less successful in its business, whose thoughts are daily familiar and their hearts daily quickened with what lies further away and higher up than plans of worldliness or schemes of ambition ever reached. If mountain-top gives clearer and ampler vision than can be had on level with fen and amidst fog, much more does the faith of humblest Christian take in what utmost grasp of worldliness cannot reach.

Such altitudes are not gained by balloon ascent, nor by mountain climbing, however much may thus be suggested. Abatement of that intense worldliness which holds the mind to such narrow range so persistently, will help a little. Instructed reason and intelligent thought can see far enough to find the utmost bounds of worldly schemes; can see where they must end; can see in what restrictions a soul must be, shut up within the narrow range traversed by men of the world, and can see what infinite possibilities lie beyond. But further on, beyond the range of worldly plans, beyond utmost scope of the senses, beyond the restrictions in which life is here held, in those regions beyond the grave, which the imagination can fill with such opposite possibilities, there and then what is to be found can be discovered only by faith. What so distant in the future, what so far away, as to be beyond the telescopic vision of faith? Whatever concerns the soul must be within reach of ultimate discovery. Faith finds all forces, all existences, constituting the universe, or presiding over its destiny, and leads the soul into adjustment with these. Such is the range and work of faith; such the mount of vision on which the believing stand. Beyond the field of knowledge, beyond the realm of reason, faith searches; in the light of God's truth and upon warrant of God's word, it makes discovery of whatever concerns the soul in the hereafter and the beyond.

Not only does the soul gain a mount of vision having such wide survey, but finds itself in fellowship with apostles, prophets, and the Son of God. A cloud of such great glory overshadows the believer that he says: "It is good to be here." Here would he build tabernacles and make his abode. Here he beholds all things in God's true perspective. Now he sees the business of the world, all the affinities and responsibilities of life, in their true relation. What all things are for, their agency in disciplining the soul, the contribution they make to human salvation, the overthrow of the Kingdom of Evil and the establishment of the Kingdom of Righteousness, become intelligible to the believer, while upon that mount of transfiguration to which faith lifts him.

Some, O, how many! never come upon any mount of transfiguration, into the brightness of no divine truth, into the glory of no divine revealment, and into the joy of no divine fellowship. What their senses certify, what they find out by processes of knowledge, — with these they have to do; what lies beyond is to them a blank. They have no world save that which comes to them through the senses; to them there are no forces or beings except such as they can measure and count by their methods of knowledge. They see not to the boundary of the morass in which they live; cannot penetrate the fog in which they are enveloped. When ambition, by the luck of fortune, helps them upon some bog above the general level, they alternate their complacent pride with pity for perhaps some commercially unfortunate Christian, who, nevertheless, lives in a world of truth, beauty, and blessedness of which they never dreamed.

Count those who live in fogs and fens, in the morass of mere worldliness, whose utmost bounds of thought and reach of aim lie not beyond business; count those who have never come upon any mountain-top view of life, and who never went up upon any mount of transfiguration, and the success of the Kingdom of Evil will be no matter of surprise.

CHAPTER XIX.

IDOLATRY OF GENIUS.

BETWEEN the Kingdom of Evil and the Kingdom of Righteousness the matter of obstinate and irreconcilable dispute is, What are the conditions of highest good and welfare? In the Kingdom of Righteousness these are affirmed to be justice, truth, love, sincerity, faithfulness, purity, and all other right principles and holy affections found in the organization of God's moral government, and adherent in his character. Such is the make of the soul, such its wants and powers, such its reason and conscience; that only when character is based on these fundamental principles of God's moral government, and shaped by them, are highest good and welfare reached. Profoundest study of the soul reveals this more clearly, and widest research makes it more indisputable.

Passing from the study of an individual soul to society, or to souls in their relations, these principles are seen to harmonize every interest, call out every power, meet every want, and secure highest welfare to each and all. Under the sway of these principles no weakest can be down-trodden, no poorest starved, none wronged; the capacity of each, on all levels, is fully met. Under acceptance of these principles of God's moral government all this must be; otherwise, utterly impossible.

To this the Kingdom of Evil demurs. It takes no flat-footed stand of honesty, affirming that wrong is right; sin, the safest guide; autonomy, better than law. There is a befoolment impossible, even to blinded men. So matters are taken up at a remove from such a centre. Mammonism is only prudence wisely looking out for the future; restless ambition is only making the most of one's self; so good taste stops not short of pride; desire for food and drink runs to animalism and debauchery, and love to licentiousness; so troop in the whole array of the world's sins, vices, and crimes, each under leadership of some justification, and maintaining very remote relations to some virtue. Principles of action, aims of pursuit, modes of conduct, and fashion of character are justified, if possible, by some plausibility, chosen and stuck to any way; all of which are against the righteousness, justice, truth, love, purity, and faithfulness, enjoined under the moral government of God; and equally against the highest welfare of the soul, and the best ordering of society. A totally different outlook of life is gained; a totally different judgment of man's normal character is formed; a totally different view is held of his relations; a totally different estimate of the wants and powers of the soul is maintained; and a totally different forecasting of the future is indulged, from what would be, under acceptance of the facts and truths of God's moral government.

That man is a sinner is denied; he is only suffering under ignorance, lack of culture, and from unfavorable surroundings. What is abnormal, is accounted for by bad digestion, mal-formed brain, inheritance of vicious temperament, defective training, and untoward example. Sin, if admitted, is minified, and held capable of management under hygiene and skilful moralities. So no room is left for the gospel, with its scheme of redemption; no need of regeneration and sanctification by a divine power. With emphasis is denial made of any such destiny and allotment of souls as is affirmed in Divine Revelation. The strictest in the Kingdom of Evil allow only such allotment hereafter as is now made by the general judgment of society. To shut men of wealth out of heaven, they say, will never do. If reminded of the grinding oppressions and corrupt practices by which that wealth has been gained, and of the oppressive ways in which it has been used, consent is readily got that some rich men should go to hell; but surely not the rich that are also respectable. Society pays court to such here, and, forsooth, must there.

To none does this class of thinkers, in their self-caring ways, pay more respect than to men of genius, men who by their inborn gifts have risen high in the world's esteem, and have written their names indelibly on the world's memory. Not to make room for all such in heaven, is their sufficient condemnation of the gospel.

This Idolatry of Genius is an element of success in the Kingdom of Evil. It is representative of a way of thinking pervading all the heights, if not all the ranges of that Kingdom, in flat contradiction, and in irreconcilable opposition, to all that is affirmed in the Kingdom of Righteousness. It demands a reconstruction of religious systems, insisting that something more, and else, than moral character shall be taken into account, in determining the eternal issues of life; that judgment at the final assize shall be held as society now holds it; that heaven shall be open to all who have access to good society here.

This looks fair to human eyes; for there is something exalted in genius. It gives one a sense of comfort and dignity to belong to a race in which are men and women of such towering genius as the world has known. In their attainments and achievements we see what reach human thoughts can have; how great a soul can be. The men who have opened to us the higher ranges of science, explored the outlying fields of astronomy, discovered a planet by the subtleties of mathematics, told us of the materials which enter into the combustion of sun and more distant star, let us into the mysteries of the microscopic world, spoken to us of the laws and forms of life in ocean beds, read to us from rocky tablets the legends of geologic revolutions in ages lying far beyond the chronologist's record; the men who have harnessed for man's use the most subtle and potent agencies of nature, opened ways for speech through ocean beds, and ways for travel across continents, surmounting all barriers of desert and mountain; the men who have risen to command and authority in the army and nation, guiding the one to victory and the other to safety, when destruction to both seemed impending;

the men who, when and where such things were possible, have built up a dynasty, holding the reins of power through many generations, and by their word bringing peace or war; the men and women who, in poetry, music, painting, sculpture, architecture, and adjacent realms of art, have brought us ideals of beauty, harmony, order, and proportion; those who have fathomed for us the profoundest depths of philosophy and the deepest mysteries of faith, shaping the world's thinking for ages; and, too, the men and women, who by creations of their genius have touched the world's heart, made it weep over the down-trodden, stirred through the nation, and beyond, a pity that would not rest till the cry for justice was lost in the shout of emancipation; men and women who in fiction have presented the highest ideals into which human character can be wrought, attracting the world's attention, fascinating its admiration; and most of all, softening the world's heart towards God's poor; if these may not go to heaven, who may?

Such question comes to us from the Kingdom of Evil, now because so respectable as to challenge admiration. And the question is backed up with the more defiant one: What will your heaven be without them? The case is stated in its strength, because to many minds there is strength in it,—felt all the more as a list of the world's geniuses is taken up, their names read off, and their achievements for humanity recalled. Here, three things require attention.

1. Not all men of genius are shut out of the Kingdom of Righteousness, and, therefore, not out of heaven. For otherwise, Religion consists with the

highest genius. Not only is it an added glory, but essential to the highest reach of genius. For what has genius to do, or ever has done, than to handle the realities of fact, thought, and feeling? And these in their highest forms and broadest relations are included in religion, which is only the fitting adjustment of the soul to these just named realities. No reality of fact, thought, and feeling can be understood in isolation, only in its surroundings and relations. God left out of account, no fact of nature or history, no thought of mind or feeling of heart, can be fully understood. He who knows not God, knows not anything as it can be known. Whatever Dickens — and the same may be said of many another genius — may have been as a man, as a writer he was not religious; he took not in what was truest and grandest concerning humanity. When his genius soared to its greatest height, it only showed how much greater he might have been, if he had only studied human character and society from that point in which he would have seen them in their relations to God. We admire his genius only to lament that it had such narrow range. Had he studied society in the height, breadth, and depth of religious thought and feeling, there would have been added an element of the infinite to the productions of his genius, which now, conceived in all their reach, are confined within very narrow bounds, having to do with man simply as a dweller on this earth. If he had found a place for the Infinite and Eternal in his works, they would have reached such immortality as human restrictions allow.

There is no such element of enlargement or factor

of multiplication, as religion affords to genius, whatever its sphere. No genius can be what is possible, without religion. He needs it not merely as the highest philosophy, in which all things find their culmination, and apart from which they are seen only in piecemeal; but in his loftiest flight he needs the inspiration of religious thought and feeling to bring him into truest appreciation and to fullest mastery of whatever he essays to handle. The irreligious genius presents things only in appearance in temporal relations, at best only in isolation; not in their profoundest reality and widest relations; for then would he have to take all greatest realities of religion into the field of his thought. So there is an element of incompleteness — and that means weakness — in his works, which leads to the decay and oblivion to which they are doomed.

This is not bald affirmation; it is the world's vote, the pronouncement of history. As a class, religious names have an immortality reached by no other. These are the names of highest chronology. "The sweet Singer of Israel," and the "Apostle to the Gentiles," were not the only men of genius in their ages. Yet David and Paul have, to-day, a place in more hearts, do more to shape the thoughts and feelings of humanity, than ever before, than all their cotemporary men of genius in the Kingdom of Evil. Indeed, though known to students, what knows or cares the world for their cotemporaries? And this place David and Paul hold, not simply by their inspiration of God, which the Kingdom of Evil denies, but, in part, because of their sanctified genius. They took in the meaning of providence and history; they saw all things in their relations to the sublime purposes God is working out; they accepted the situation,—man a sinner, Christ a gracious Saviour. Their genius made them what they were, because it was inspired by religious faith and sanctified by holy love. But for this, history would have left them in the oblivion where rest their cotemporary men of genius in the Kingdom of Evil, now known, if at all, only as forming the necessary background in the scenes of their heroic action, or as flies in amber.

For men of sanctified genius, humanity has prepared and preserves a niche as for no others, because men were made to be religious. Nothing so normal as that. The quailing eye of the wrong-doer, the blush of shame, and the rebuke of conscience tell that men were not made to sin. Men must be true to their nature, and cherish carefulest and longest the works of genius that have brought closest to their hearts the sublime realities of faith. It is humiliating to take up a biographical dictionary, and see in what brief paragraphs the world's great men are disposed of. Little concerning them is of interest after a few centuries. Admiring the monuments that preserve their names, men have to inquire who they were and what they did. Not so with men of genius that have quickened the world's religious aspirations, helped its deliverance from sin, and lifted humanity Godward.

There are men of genius who have not done this, as the world knows too well; men who have prostituted high gifts of genius to the bewilderment and corruption of men; have thrown a fascinating charm over all ways of evil; given a phosphorescent glare of brilliancy to foulest corruptions; made vice beautiful; given sin what dignity it could bear, and besmirched virtue as best they could. To give their names and tell wherein would only justify and intensify this charge. If in the galaxy of sanctified genius in heaven, such be wanting, it will be all the more resplendent.

2. Some simplest truth often settles gravest matters. No endowment of wit or brilliancy of conversational powers would be the necessary qualification of an engineer driving the train on which we ride. Skill in poetic or musical composition commend no one as a legal adviser. When disease is doing its work of destruction with our loved ones, we inquire not for a physician best known for skill in metaphysical casuistry. No profoundness of erudition in abstract science would give us confidence in the leader of an army. Strength of muscle and athletic skill are not what we seek in a religious instructor. All the way through, and in every condition, we demand attainments that shall give fit qualification.

So genius fits not for heaven. As well admit one on the bulk of his estate, the height of his stature, his skill in athletics, or the reach of his longevity. Fiction and poetry are forms of thought, and, to be commended or condemned, account must be taken of their contents. So genius is skill and power, and, for commendation or condemnation, respect must be had to what it does. Genius runs in all directions, through all ranges of knowledge and art. It may be in skill of eye, ear, voice, or fingers. Look at the bounds of its range; subtlest metaphysical inquiry, utmost research of science, thorough analysis of human nature, skill in arts constructive, musical, poetical, and fictional, in æsthetics, in military affairs and monetary, down to skill in games, chances, and horse-flesh. The world has made boast of its geniuses in all these departments, and lower. Gather all these men and women of genius, with their pride and passion and nervous particularity, into a world by themselves, with such surroundings as their gifts require, and what kind of a heaven would it be?

The universe is for something, and so is this life. And the issues which eternity contains, and which it alone can contain, are that something. That highest end is moral, simply because the moral includes all things else. The soul to be right morally, religiously, or spiritually, requires exclusion of defect in all other ranges of its being. Whatever genius has reached, or has done, only met the moral requirement in part. These men of genius proved themselves worthy of the world's admiration by noteworthy development in some single direction, that is only part in that complete and full-orbed life which meets the moral requirement. Genius is only excrescent, partial, and incomplete; and if, as too often, out of harmony with moral obligation, it is wanting in the essentials of highest life, and is unadjusted to the realities and uses of the universe.

God is the greatest reality, — more than he has made, more than he has done. Out of harmony with him, opposed to his moral government, antagonistic to the principles of justice, righteousness, love, faith, purity, and holiness enjoined in his word; in denial of the gospel's facts, that man is a sinner and Christ a Saviour; whatever else genius can be, it is lacking in adjustment to the central and greatest realities of the universe; and even by the laws of order and fitness it must go with the defective. Holiness is the law of heaven, love its pervading spirit, Christ its central glory, and whatever fails to harmonize with these cannot have place or fellowship there.

3. Holiness of moral character is the highest type and measure of man. In God, infinite truth, power, goodness, purity, wisdom, love, and whatever other glory or perfection the mind can conceive, find their exhaustless source and perfect illustration. Highest development of genius, even if sanctified by loyalty to God, is only some small approach Godward, on a low level and within narrow range. "Nearer, my God, to Thee," is a cry for greatness, the highest a soul can reach.

It is no arbitrary enactment that opens heaven only to souls loving God, believing in Christ, repenting of sin, and hungering after righteousness. Such accept the situation, themselves lost in sin, and Christ the only Saviour. In faith they open their hearts Godward, and receive what God has to give. Comprehensively, it is a new life. It recreates the soul, unites it to God, gives the soul God's thoughts, principles, spirit, and feelings, and lifts the soul into fellowship with God in views, aims, and desires. Here is the germ of a new life, to be unfolded eternally; and in its unfolding will be included all that is possible to a soul, — a reach of thought, a comprehension of truth, an appreciation of beauty in all forms and of harmony in all combinations, a recip rocation of love, a power of accomplishment, and a flow of enjoyment, beyond reach of any genius yet, or of all combined. The Christian life is the highest any soul can have, for it includes germinally all a soul can be, do, or enjoy. Rudimentally, the Christian is the highest genius.

Many do not receive this. The men of the world do not. We know their blindness too well to expect it. They take entirely different views. To them, what is even a respectable and obvious Christian, compared with any whom the world has learned to admire as a genius? Yet the world's genius in poetry may be a libertine; the world's genius in fiction may shorten his life in intemperate and over-fed animalism; the world's kings may be debauchees. For safety the world may have to imprison its greatest military genius on an ocean island; and the name of its monetary genius may be a synonyme for rascality.

But men of the world will admire their men of genius for all that. In comparison, what is the most indisputable Christian? With what an air of contempt they behold it, if a Christian is put in comparison with any of their men of genius! And if the presumption be pressed, how ready are they with their scorn! Heaven must be opened to their men of genius, how many soever Christians may have to vacate.

And yet the simplest, humblest Christian has in his soul, by virtue of his union with God, and the inflowing of a divine life, the germ of all angelic strength, beauty, and greatness. He may be trammelled with many an ignorant prejudice, held under power of narrow views and low habits, may be very ignorant of the ways of the world, of the facts of nature and the truths of science. After learning the way of gaining a cheap livelihood, he may not know more than to feed his soul with some simplest truths of God's word; to draw near to his Saviour in penitent trust and prayer, and to show his love for man by acts whose only value lay in their kind intent. Dwarf him down to smallest pattern of manhood, make him the butt of ridicule, a standing laughing-stock, utterly unable to appreciate men of genius; in a spirit of caste put upon him all the indignities of prejudice and hate, and leave him to wriggle out of his difficulties as best he can; yet in God's view,—somewhat clearer and broader than that of the men of the world,—there is in this man's soul capacities far transcending the gifts of genius, the germ of powers equalled only by an angel's. This God sees as clearly as we can see the oak in the germinate acorn. That marred and deflected image of Christ, which unspiritualized vision cannot see, Christ can; and more, he has identified himself with that lowly believer, so that "inasmuch as ye did it not to him" in his need, ye did it not to Christ. The name of that believer, standing low in the world's esteem, stands on record in the Lamb's Book of Life.

"Pursuit of heaven under difficulties,"—the world may say. Yea, more than that, under impossibilities, if the way were to be found by his knowledge, the achievement to be made by his wisdom, and the victory gained by his strength. But for victory, for completed salvation, he has given himself in perfect trust and confiding love to the keeping of a Heavenly Father, who will not leave him to perish, more than a mother her child with rescue within reach. It is no arbitrary appointment, only the natural issue of things, that heaven's gate should be open to any humblest believer in Christ.

Right with God, right in moral character, harmoniously adjusted into the soul's true relations, accepting what Christ in his plan of salvation has provided and in his grace has offered, only time, opportunity, favoring conditions, and the maintained life of God in the soul, are needed to make that soul right, complete, harmonized, and matured in all the lengths, breadths, heights, and depths of his being; transcending all reach of genius, soaring with angels to all heights of knowledge, and entering into fellowship with God, both in thought and feeling.

Marred to utter spoiling are all who come short of this. Not adjusted to God in the way the gospel provides, they are out of harmony with the eternal laws and highest uses of the universe, out of adjustment with all its forces, out of conditions of highest and eternal welfare, and in oppugnance with reason and conscience. The vital elements of soul-life are wanting, moral recovery and moral adjustment. Genius cannot save them; as well expect beauty of face to ward off disease, or a metaphysical argument to arrest the work of death.

But, in exact accordance with the blindness and

bewilderment of sin, the men of the world, in their idolatry of genius, take no such view of the matter; they will not brook the idea that men of genius should fail of entrance into heaven; that they should fail of whatever goodness and glory the future world has. To a great majority of unbelieving men, this would not seem a question of practical importance. But it accords with their vanity, that each should count himself a genius by some method of measurement; so they hold the question practical to themselves. At least, they put forth the army of gifted unbelievers as a forlorn hope, whose success may gain them entrance. They mean that heaven shall be open to all who have access to good society here, and good society is their society. They put forward the world's men of genius, as if, beyond dispute, heaven could not do without them; so they hope room will be made for all.

They demand a reconstruction of religious systems, and insist that the judgment of the world shall be the arbiter of final destiny; that other measures of judgment than moral character shall be applied; that the fact of sin shall be ignored; that the need of redemption and recovery shall not be insisted upon. This sentiment, so congenial to the human heart, this feeling, so pervasive in the world, is an element of success in the Kingdom of Evil, likely to entrap many heedless and unwary souls.

CHAPTER XX.

PERSONAL HISTORY AND CHARACTER.

THE Elements of Success in the Kingdom of Evil, hitherto considered, are convictions, impulses, and moral disturbances, working general derangement in society, corrupting its spirit, lowering its tone, and creating a bad atmosphere. Living in this general distemperature, in such unhealthy conditions, congenial to latent depravity, all souls become diseased in their action, whatever their original constitution.

Of these general causes, there are others working derangement in ways more or less direct, and helping the Kingdom of Evil to success. Having already overgone the length designed, these are left without even enumeration, to look briefly into the realm of personal history and character, without which the subject gets no full treatment.

As minds take in what they will naturally absorb of the malign influences before noted, they not only hold them in different quantities, but make diverse selections, according to original bias, or as determined by some event or condition of early life. These generally give positiveness of character and

16

even idiosyncracies. Few come to adult life without showing some characteristic perversity, well known to acquaintances, which is an obstacle in the way of escape from the Kingdom of Evil, and thus an element of its success.

The variety and shading of these personal peculiarities reach towards the infinite; no two alike, more than faces. One of a sort is enough. No description, or even enumeration, of them is possible; yet they are only varieties and modifications of a few cardinal perversities, like the varieties of nature from a few chemical simples. Consideration can here be afforded only for some of those seed vices whose outgrowths are so numerous and varied.

Every study of the soul reveals manifold reasons why all men should be Christians, fully delivered out of the Kingdom of Evil and safely included in God's Kingdom of Righteousness. Reasons, however invalid, there must be, why they are not. These are obstacles hindering the escape of all those yet in the Kingdom of Evil. What these hinderances are, and how valid, as a matter of personal concern, few inquire. They are unable to give any intelligent justification of their position, yet they stay in it most immovably. Of this, where cannot illustration be found? We inquire for those hinderances which bar escape from the Kingdom of Evil, as found in personal history and character.

1. The sway of some appetite or lust. That many are under such control, is painfully evident to one who has given any study to the condition and phases of society. What these appetites and lusts

will lead men to do, is utterly incredible to one who has given no study to their history. In sacrifice thereto there have been laid on the altar, wealth, health, position in society, success in life, all that men usually toil and struggle for. The mind is wearied and palled with surprises and astonishments at the power which lusts and appetites have over men; it would seem that, acted out as vices, they could exhibit no new monstrosity capable of exciting wonder.

And how safely included in the Kingdom of Evil are the men over whom they dominate. The level on which such a man lives, the atmosphere he breathes, the views of life familiar to him, the companionship he enjoys, and the aims he seeks, bring him into affinity and fellowship with evil. In his temper, modes of thought, and moods of feeling, he invites no saving influence of the gospel to reach and rectify him. If his aim had been to make his position in the Kingdom of Evil impregnable, he could not have done better. Hedged about, as so many are, with vices, and dominated over by lusts, they give the Kingdom of Evil all the success their numbers can afford.

2. The overgrowth of some ambition. Many have such intelligent views of life, such a sense of decency and self-respect, that they keep themselves aloof and above vice. The bewilderment of intoxication, the animalism of debauchery, and the craze of gambling, have no attractions for them. They are too wary for spendthrift vices, too prudent for those which are corrupting, and too self-respectful for those which

are debasing. These are the decent men that make up the bulk of society. Yet in just these often is found the overgrowth of some ambition. In early life some incident fired their ambition, that has grown with their growth.

One has been humiliated with poverty, or has been brought into some distress thereby. To escape from such woes, he has resolved to gain the power of wealth, not as a means of beneficence, but to environ himself with power. For this, nothing is permitted to stand in the way; no hinderance of moral principle, no better use of his powers, no courtesy of life, no disrepute, no endangerment of health, or possibly evaded criminality of law, will he allow to abate his struggle for wealth.

The pride of another has been touched. Social caste has stung him with its scorn. From such exposure he resolves to escape at any cost. If to gain position in what is called "fashionable life," slaving for wealth, hard study, and the severe practice of accomplishments be necessary, time and effort will be given to these. In many a school of culture, as in many a place of business, will be found such aspirants. But if there be no taste or genius for accomplishments, cheaper methods will be adopted. The regalia of fashionable dress is put upon the body, whatever offence be thus given to correct taste. The furniture and appointments of home must be of latest style; and old but well-kept furniture, rich in dear associations of domestic life, must go to auction rooms and there lose their history. Worried with this strain after appearances, vain of whatever success is reached, puffed up with the admiring gaze of the silly, by the buzz of talk they make in resorts where fashion airs herself, and perhaps by the gossip of tattling newspapers, fired with such an ambition, breathing such an atmosphere, no living inspiration of the gospel can reach them; and so they give all the success to the Kingdom of Evil that froth and frivolity can.

Political ambition, or professional, has inoculated others with its virus. To reach the heights of power, or to be renowned in their calling, men have sacrificed whatever stood in the way. If they aspired to be at the head of the nation, to tread the halls of congress, to hold office in state or county, however high their ambition, or low, they are in contest for power. They want elevation, perhaps for mere self-aggrandizement, perhaps to tyrannize over their fellows; for the love of power is congenial to the natural heart; in a thousand houses there is tyranny enough wasted, which, had it concentration, could devastate the land with wars.

There are men of even balance, whom no such ambitions disturb. Others, of such broad and clear views of life, of such generous spirit and Christian principle, that they are free from the all-devouring greed of personal ambition; others escape such peril simply by being drones. But large numbers are left, who are filled with strong or weak ambitions. These put what powers they have to such stretch, nurse in themselves such egoism, as to keep them aloof from the gospel, and help the Kingdom of Evil to success.

3. Unsuccessful attempts at being religious. Few

men come to adult life without having made some attempt at being religious. It may have been under very unfavorable circumstances. Antecedent education may not have given them any true or well-defined conception of the object to be reached. Indeed, so confused are the minds of many, that they have no intelligent notion of what it is to be religious; so blinded are some, that, were they to become Christians, they would not know the fact, nor be able to tell what had been done in its accomplishment; and this confusion of thought helps the Kingdom of Evil.

Not knowing what is done in becoming religious, they have no intelligent conception of the ways and means of reaching that end; so that, however sincere their purpose may be, their misapprehension of ways and means is likely to bar them from any desirable result. Many undertake to be religious from fear of consequences, or from pressure of a guilty conscience. The attempt lacks consideration; is impulsive, and likely to be misguided. They do what they see others do, yet without apprehending their inward experience, and so fail in the chief thing. They have the fears which trouble others, have the emotions of guilt which others describe, and the purposes of obedience which others express. Borne along in the tide of feeling in which others participate, they are willing to do many acts commonly regarded characteristically Christian. Their emotions of fear and sorrow having subsided, as all emotions will, they infer that their calmness, instead of being exhaustion, is some rude form of peace and joy. With others they join the church; not that they would have thought of so doing from their own wants or felt attractions; not to make good their professions; not to give proof of their sincerity, and to put themselves in the way of an earnest Christian life; but simply because others join the church; and because, being Christians, they suppose that is the way to do.

Accepting the judgment of the church on the doubtful question of their piety, they imagine they are now to move smoothly on in the Christian way. When the contests of the Christian warfare begin, when they are set to the disruption of former habits and mastery of favorite sins, they find that a human will, even when strengthened by pride of consistency, is too weak for control of sin. They give way to former indulgences in evil, and show themselves to be what all along they had been,— fast in their original unconversion. Whether they have gone so far as to join the church, or had a less pronounced turn at being religious, they give proof to others, and are compelled at length to accept it themselves, that the root of the matter is not in them.

Having passed through such an experience, some are utterly discouraged, thinking that a Christian life is beyond their reach; others have willingly wronged their consciences, and are both sore and repugnant at all approaches of the gospel; others feel that they have made fools of themselves, and are determined to guard against like exposure hereafter by keeping wholly aloof from the gospel. So they give bulk and corresponding success to the Kingdom of Evil.

Were all men's biographies published, and the secret history of their hearts brought to light, perhaps in every community would be found some who had made a most unfortunate attempt in being religious. By their failure they have placed themselves aloof from Christian influence, in antagonism to the gospel; perhaps have deliberately made up their minds never again to attempt a religious life. They have exhausted their religious sensibility, blinded their minds, deadened their consciences, hardened their hearts, weakened the faith of others in respect to them, and created a past whose historic influences turn them away from the Christian path. To them, religion is either impracticable, a delusion, or a matter of luck and chance, and they are not backward in uttering their convictions. Of the elements of success in the Kingdom of Evil, which the numbers and influence of such are, every church is painfully aware.

4. Early training in loose morality. It is difficult to determine where is the turning-point which practically settles a soul's destiny for salvation or ruin. In general, it is, consciously and obviously, in the experience of conversion, or in the soul's last rejection of God's offered mercy. Ordinarily, it is when a soul purposely relies on the mercy of God in Christ Jesus, or chooses to take the risk of not doing so; it is when a soul decides to be an obedient, or an incorrigibly rebellious subject of God's moral government.

But when that question consciously comes up for settlement under the pressure of truth and the striving of God's Spirit, how it shall issue may practically have been determined long before, yea, in early life, in some conflict of the child with parental authority. How the mind will act under the pressure of religious obligation, how loyal it will be to truth, how sensitive and authoritative conscience will be, these are matters often settled in early life; and when once settled, determine, at least go far to settle, the action of the soul, when it takes up for settlement, as a law of life, the question of loyalty or disloyalty to God.

Let a child be trained into loose moralities, into ways that violate conscience, that make his mind dishonest to truth, disloyal to obligation, and apart from the evil habits thus begotten, which fence his way of return to righteousness, his habits of mind, the whole run of his moral nature contributes to the success of the Kingdom of Evil.

When we look into the current life of children and youth, see how many of them devoid of religious culture are not held by their parents even to such moralities as are necessary for the comfort of the family; how imperious wilfulness, not yet tempered by reason and reflection, sways them as passion or pleasure dictates, and how loose are the moralities into which they grow, we find painful augury that the success to which the Kingdom of Evil has reached is likely to be continued in the next generation.

5. The power of habit. It is a familiar thing in the experience of all adults, that they have fallen into modes of thought, feeling, speech, and conduct that are characteristic. The gait of some tell who they are, when too distant to discern the face.

Methods of thought reveal authorship. Tones and inflections of voice, even out of natural pitch, reveal the speaker in the dark. Moral conduct gets into the same fixed and positive ways. Thus fashioned and hardened under long experience in sin, this rigidity of habit becomes almost an insuperable bar to religious life. If overcome so far as to enter the Christian way, how often is the young Christian found running in the grooves of his former life. He is not less pained than surprised at the oath which his lips utter so instinctively, at the imperiousness of his resents, and at the congeniality with which he drops into his former habits of sin.

To one who knows the power of habit by any attempt at revolution, it stands before him as one ot the obstacles to entrance on a religious life that it will require changes, to be opposed at every step by the obstinacy of habit. The uncomfortableness of disturbing these habits, doubts about success in it, and the disrepute of failure, hold many a man fast in the Kingdom of Evil. The longer he stays, every added year gives greater rigidity to habits and environs him more completely in their power, so that this obstinacy of habit gives stability to the success the Kingdom of Evil has gained.

6. Misapprehended or false testimony of church members. Some who have made no attempt at being religious, and so come to no failure in it, have had an experience equally disastrous, though not so destructive of personal integrity. They have been deceived by the misapprehended or false testimony of church members. This testimony may have

seemed false to their minds, merely because they misapprehended its facts and spirit. All that was said and done by the Christian witness, they have not known. Its essential spirit and meaning they have not caught. They have not submitted the testimony to cross-examination. What seemed unchristian and weakened their faith in religion, would have had an entirely different aspect, could they have known all about the facts, the witness, and especially the inside of his life. Or the testimony may have been positively false; given either by a hypocrite, or by one who at length proves himself a real Christian, though in the matter in hand acting ignorantly, under the bias of prejudice, or in a state of lamentable declension. Wide extremes in moods and frames of feeling, the sway of diverse principles, entertainment of very different views, and exposure to widely various influences, are common to all men. From these the Christian is not exempt. Such extremes are in human nature, in the run of life, and religion does not immediately exclude them.

So both by the hypocrite and imperfect Christian, sometimes by an entire church, wrongs have been done, wrongs in the matter of reputation, requiring the testimony of years of faithful living to secure rectification; wrongs in the matter of property, amounting sometimes to an oppression of the weak and defenceless; wrongs that have despoiled the widow of home and the fatherless of inheritance; wrongs that have blasted reputation, that have crushed hopes, sacrificed virtue, separated husband and wife, broken up families, and sent the injured to a speedy grave. These wrongs have been committed by those who stood representatives, perhaps public advocates, of religion. And while their inflicted suffering continues, or even a remembrance of it, the false dilemma in which the sufferers and their friends have permitted themselves to be placed, is, — either that religion allowed such things, or else is a delusion, in not having power to prevent them.

Such wrongs might be expected in a world where ignorance and misconception, both of facts and motives, prevail, and where sin works so freely. And the consequent misapprehensions we may expect in the Kingdom of Evil. And thousands there are today, whom the sufferance of such wrongs, real or imaginary, has maddened against the Christian religion in a way beyond probable pacification. They hold religion, its Sabbaths, its professors, its ministers, its worshipping assemblies, and its sacraments, in fancied contempt and positive hatred. They have barred all escape for themselves from the Kingdom of Evil. Scarcely immoralities and foulest vices could place them further from the Kingdom of Righteousness. That to the Kingdom of Evil such should be an element of success is no matter of dispute or surprise.

7. Then a large number are blinded as to the nature and necessity of religion. There is no high and grand theme, capable of taxing all highest powers of mind and touching all deepest feelings of heart, to a true and full knowledge of which men come by instinct and without study. Such a matter is religion. And although to all sincere and rightly-

acting minds intent upon being true to themselves in the highest relations of life, the substantial verities of religion are within reach, yet such minds are few. By the many, religion is not understood in its nature and necessity, because they give it no candid and earnest study. Banishing from their minds the infinite realities that are around them, looking not upward to what is above them, nor forward to what is before them, forgetting all highest relations and deepest wants of the soul, they can, in ordinary conditions, live very comfortable lives without religion; so they give it little thought and less study.

Upon few minds come not some shading of this darkness. In its penumbra, if not in its densest shadow, can be found men of high culture and women of great brilliancy. This fact is a part of sin's curse, — its cause in part. If the Kingdom of Evil is to have success, here we might expect to find one element of it.

It would confuse to detail all these facts of personal history and character which give success to the Kingdom of Evil. By some evil companionship, casually formed and soon ripened into maturity, one and another is held fast in the Kingdom of Evil. Manifold debasing pleasures, vast array of demoralizing art, floods of corrupting literature, — O, the world is full of the enginery of evil!

8. Mention will be made of one other fact of personal character, — obstinacy of will. It is difficult for some men to get their own consent to any change in their thoughts, feelings, plans, or conduct, however urgent the reasons. They have no grace

of pliancy. The cast-iron rigidity of their wills holds them fast to the evil into which they first were moulded. Only by refusion and remoulding can they be changed. They hold on to a course, simply because they have set their faces in that direction, even after they see the folly of it. A determination once formed, they count as so much capital invested; and if the speculation be clearly seen unprofitable, they hold it as a matter of honesty with themselves to carry it through and take the consequences. They may as well be left to their course, for persuasion is as vain as if expended on the law of gravity. Pity they could not have been started right, then might the world have seen the perfect steadfastness of uprightness.

But starting in the wrong way, their immovable obstinacy gives stability to the Kingdom of Evil. They came into that Kingdom by inheritance; and though far from its deep corruptions and wild fanaticisms, though living in the moralities that border the adjacent Kingdom of Righteousness, they cannot be induced either to abandon the Kingdom of Evil, or to enter more heartily into its spirit and design, simply because they never permit themselves to be persuaded out of their course. No one knows the rigidity of an obstinate will, unless he has expended all the arguments of the gospel, and all the tender anxieties of a Christian heart, in the vain attempt to turn such an one to Christ. In this he gets a meaning of the word *impossible* never before conceived. Once converted, these men make their obstinacy of will, somewhat softened, an element of strength in their Christian firmness. Otherwise they are muniments of the Kingdom of Evil, giving stability to its success.

Some obstacles or other, often more than one, hinder escape from the Kingdom of Evil in the case of vast multitudes. What thus hinders escape is a matter of such grave concern, that, judging from the importance of the matter, every sinner would be supposed to know and fully appreciate what holds him so resistlessly in subordination to the Kingdom of Evil. Seemingly, this he would find out, simply from the curiosity every man is entitled to have concerning himself. Yet the Kingdom of Evil is seldom disturbed by any such investigations.

Some of these, or like hinderances, keep the vast majority of men, hitherto, from being Christians. It may be the enormous development of some appetite, or lust; the dominant ascendency of some ambition, as for riches, power, fashion, or pleasure; some unsuccessful attempt at being religious; early training in loose morality; the power of habit; misapprehension of false testimony of church members; blindness as to the nature and necessity of religion; obstinacy of will, or other like obstacles not considered in this chapter. Hinderances there are of great force, since they hold men so firmly against reasons whose validity and importance they cannot deny. There is ample warrant for that curiosity about themselves, which shall lead them to find exactly and measure accurately the obstacles that fence them into the Kingdom of Evil, and out of the Kingdom of Christ and its great salvation.

These reasons, which keep men from the way of salvation, and the before considered elements of success in the Kingdom of Evil, awaken an inexpressible sadness in every rightly-acting mind, only to be deepened by others not taken into view. To combat these reasons, when attempted, has been wholly incidental to their full presentation. The aim has been to study the facts of the condition, and to find, as best we could, why the Kingdom of Evil, against reason, revelation, c onscience, all highest powers in man, all deepest wants of the heart, and against best welfare of society, has a success found nowhere else. The reasons given, though no justification, show how such success has come, and suggest some ways of combating it.

www.ingramcontent.com/pod-product-compliance
Lightning Source LLC
LaVergne TN
LVHW050514100826
845148LV00002B/332

* 9 7 8 1 4 2 5 5 2 1 8 5 1 *